VINTAGE

restaurant

VINTAGE

restaurant

handcrafted cuisine from
a sun valley favorite

.....

JEFF KEYS

PHOTOGRAPHY BY GLEN ALLISON

Gibbs Smith, Publisher
Salt Lake City

First Edition
10 09 08 07 06   5 4 3 2 1

Text © 2006 Jeff Keys
Photographs © 2006 Glen Allison

Published by
Gibbs Smith, Publisher
P.O. Box 667
Layton, Utah 84041

Orders: 1.800.748.5439
www.gibbs-smith.com

Printed and bound in Hong Kong

Library of Congress Cataloging-in-Publication Data

Keys, Jeff.
  Vintage restaurant : handcrafted cuisine from a sun valley favorite / Jeff Keys ; photographs by Glen Allison.—1st ed.
    p. cm.
  ISBN 1-58685-771-1
  1. Cookery, American. I. Title.

TX715.K424 2006
641.5973—dc22

2005035085

contents

■ ■ ■ ■

SALADS AND DRESSINGS 55

The Lost Art of Great Soup 79

Tomato Manifesto 101

Brown Sauce Interlude 116

ENTRÉES 120

Desserts
183

acknowledgments

■■■■

The creation of anything starts with the planting of a seed, whether in the ground or in the mind. With help from nature, the seed sprouts and grows into a plant, maybe a single cornstalk. Or the seed can be an idea that is written into a word that becomes a sentence, then a paragraph, and then a page. With luck and help, the cornstalk becomes a field of corn. The page becomes a chapter, then a book.

Planting the seed is where everything starts, and with that in mind I'd like to thank Gibbs Smith for discovering our little mountain civilization and giving me the opportunity to create this book. Gibbs planted the seed and I thank him for that.

Cooking keeps me disciplined and focused, but in practically everything else in life I am by nature a bit untamed, and because of that I owe a deep dept of gratitude to my editor, Jennifer Grillone, for her amazing patience and careful guidance in dealing with a man whose sense of time is more akin to wild horses.

It was always fun and a pleasure to work with my photographer, Glen Allison. Besides being good at what he does, he cares about the world we live in and brought a sense of fun to our photographic sessions. We could talk and work things out—and when I ran out of ideas Glen always had one that we could take off on. I thank him for being there.

A big thank you goes to author Wendell Berry for the knowledge and inspiration I've gleaned from his poetry and essays, and for bringing an awareness of our agriculture and our connection to the earth. His work should be required reading for all cooks, farmers, politicians, and anyone who wants this to be a better world.

And many thanks to Van Morrison for staying in touch with the spirits and accompanying me through many long afternoons of heated prep work, racing the clock to the rapidly approaching dinner hour. His music helped soothe my soul and nervous system.

I'd like to acknowledge my wife, Sheila. Thank you for having a big heart of gold and for keeping my feet planted somewhat squarely on the ground. And to my kids, Austin, Andre, and Ian, and to Adrien and Stacey from another lifetime, thank you for being filled with love and showing it in your eyes. And to my mom, Barbara—my love of good food started with you. Thanks for all of those great meals you worked so hard to create. They are embedded in my bones.

And thanks go to Robert J Conaway, Keith Olander, and Alan Krinsky, for the faith and eternal friendship no matter what the distance. Keep howling at the moon, boys!

And to the warriors of my staff—Karl, Sheila, Joyce, Cherry, Trish, Cherie, Ronny, Carmen, Edita, Austin, Ryan, and Rodrigo—you create the magic out of sheer force of will and I thank you.

A special thanks goes to Dick, Sherry, Mike, and Bob, the Leadville Limited posse and hard-nosed business achievers, for letting me be me, and for having heart and flair.

To Bill Slater, your enthusiasm for life, and your grace and elegance, have always been an inspiration to me—a light in a dark sky to look up to.

And finally, a most gracious thank you to our customers, who find their way to our door and make it all worthwhile.

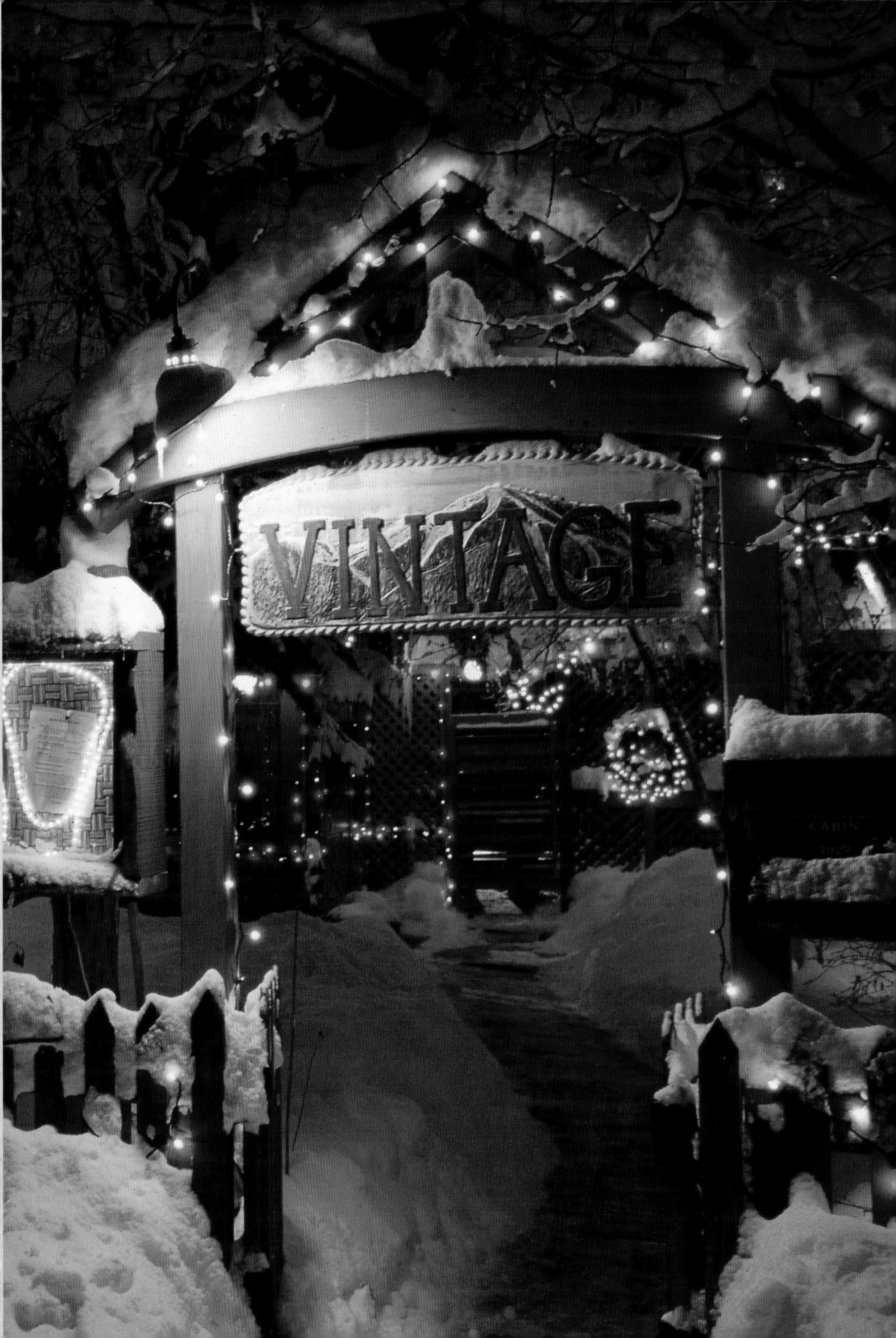
VINTAGE
CABIN

introduction

■■■■

I was raised near the ocean in Southern California. While most of the kids I was raised with were drawn to the beach, I was always looking east to the mountain ranges that surrounded Los Angeles and Orange County. First to Big Bear where my family had a cabin. Then to Convict Lake in the High Sierras with my grandparents on summer fishing and camping trips. Finally, when I discovered skiing, Mammoth Mountain became my second home.

My skiing buddies and I would drive all night on Thursday, arrive at Mammoth at 7 a.m., eat breakfast in the lodge and ski all day on Friday, Saturday, and Sunday. Then we'd hightail it back to Southern Cal on Sunday night to go back to the drudgery of school on Monday morning. It was 700 miles round trip and it didn't phase us.

I would be filled up with the energy of the mountains, the motion of skiing, the rhythm of the downhill runs, and the rage of wild blizzards. I loved it all. Watching the mountain people was fascinating to me. I wanted to stay and be one of them. It took me a while to be brave enough to do it.

In the summer of 1968 on one amazing cathartic day when I had had enough of my young life, I went to visit my grandparents at their house in Compton. I loved it there. My grandmother, Marion, made great meals. My grandfather, Clint, raised chickens and had a garden with strawberries, corn, and tomatoes. They had avocado trees, and orange and lemon trees. It was like a mini farm. They were also hunters and fishermen so they had wild game and

steelhead and tuna in the freezer. My granddad had his own sports room with all his fishing and hunting gear, special mounted antlers, and all kinds of accessories for the outdoor life. The room had its own great smell. It was my granddad.

I was sitting there that day paging through an *Arizona Highways* magazine. I came to an article on the beauty of Aspen, Colorado, in the fall. I read the article and in that exact moment, a profound feeling came over me. It became totally clear what I would do. The next day I announced to everyone in my world that I was leaving for Colorado the following night at midnight. Parents, grandparents, and friends all must have thought that I had gone off my rocker, but they gave me their blessing, thinking, I'm sure, that I would return in a short time. They were taking bets. But armed with a new sleeping bag and $100 from my grandfather, I saw the door of my life open up and I drove out of it at precisely midnight. I will never forget the feeling of exhilaration of driving away from everything I had known up to that moment and into a new life that I knew was out there somewhere. To make a long story short, I got to Aspen in two days with my VW Bug packed with everything I owned and my exhilaration now tempered with a new feeling of total panic. But I stayed on and adjusted because it was so darn beautiful in Aspen and everyone there seemed so exotic and interesting, and a totally new and unexpected life did open up to me. I discovered freedom and the possibility of being anything I wanted to be. That seemed to be the theme of being in a mountain town, and there were people there from all over the world that seemed to have the same idea. They were the people that I wanted to be with all along, and with that realization I knew I would never be going back to Southern California.

It was in Aspen in the summer of 1968 that I had my first true taste of freedom. It was a flavor I liked very much. Life in a mountain town had an energy of excitement, unpredictability and anticipation. People rich and poor, old and young, from all over the world were there because they wanted to be there. That seemed to create a bond among the citizenry and an atmosphere of kinship, adventure, and self-discovery.

One of the first things I discovered was that the local cafés and restaurants had really good food. It was food that I had never seen before. That was because of the Europeans who came to Aspen. They discovered and fell in love with our mountains after World War II. They brought their culture, skills, food, and mountain savvy to our mountain towns all over the country. Aspen was the fountainhead.

In the sixties, Aspen also became a magnet for the rich with money to burn, college kids looking for adventure, ski bums, society dropouts, artists, musicians, hippies, Hollywood stars, and—with the resort boom hitting full stride—developers and construction workers. With all the activity of growth and change, a new breed hit the mountains. Politicians and bureaucrats came out of the woodwork. It was a classic melting pot that in the summer of 1969

met a crescendo of turbulence between the forces of what Aspen had been and what it was about to become.

Being young and really more interested in the romance of Aspen, I didn't pay too much attention to the politics swirling around me. But in the fall of 1969 an event took everyone in Aspen by storm. It was the local election for county sheriff. Hunter S. Thompson, the king of gonzo journalism, decided to throw his hat into the ring against longtime Sheriff Whitmire. Now I'm sure Sheriff Whitmire was a good man, but he could not have understood the forces that were changing his county forever. He came off as a very angry man. When the debates took place that fall between Whitmire and Thompson, a circus atmosphere took over Aspen. It was like a rock concert. Everyone had to be there. I was there just to see the carnage and fireworks. Hunter Thompson was Hunter Thompson. He was funny and came at things in a way that I'm sure the good sheriff couldn't understand. That really was the whole point. Neither side could really understand the other. The worlds were just too far apart.

Those debates were a true historical watermark in Aspen. They marked the moment that Aspen changed forever. Hunter S. Thompson lost the election by nineteen votes, but Aspen changed anyway.

Besides the glorious mountains, the food world in Aspen captured my soul. The first time I ate the croissant and lightly scrambled eggs at the Epicure I knew I was in a different world. My first European pastries and soup were at a little shop called Delice. They were little pieces of art that you could eat. My first dinner at a true mountain restaurant, The Skiers Chalet, tasted so good and was so much fun it changed my brain.

My creative awareness opened up after these meals and I soon realized that I could ski every day if I got a job in one of the restaurants at night. Which, lo and behold, is what I did.

During the Christmas holidays of 1968 my best friend and co-conspirator in wild skiing and endless storytelling, Kenny Williams, got a job as a dishwasher at the Pomegranate Inn, one mile out of Aspen at the base of Buttermilk Mountain and on the edge of Art and Betty Pfisters Lazy Chair Ranch. That ranch and its owners, family, ranch foreman, and ranch hands

and horses would soon come to have a profound effect on my life. But I didn't know that yet and it is a story for another time.

That first night after Kenny worked, he came home and said they needed another dishwasher. So the next night I showed up for work and became happily ensconced at the dishwasher station where Kenny and I, being young and hungry and of a going-for-it spirit, proceeded to do a great job and also eat more prime rib than any two people on earth.

The Pomegranate Inn was not one of Aspen's temples of gourmet cuisine. It was essentially a steak house and prime rib parlor with a huge salad bar. But it was the quintessential ski area restaurant and lodge that needed young ski bums to work the low-paying service jobs like dishwashers and maids. They also had a basement boiler room and they let Kenny and me move into it for free and sleep on cots with our sleeping bags. The Pomegranate became our home. We felt like kings. Up early for breakfast in the restaurant kitchen, the morning chef more than willing to feed us anything we wanted. The owner of the Pomegranate, Dan Weigner, had given us both ski passes to Aspen Highlands, so we'd go skiing till about 3 in the afternoon and be back to work about 3:30. We'd work and eat until about 11:30 p.m. and then go swimming in the pool or take a sauna and then hang out in the bar with the clientele until late. Could being a ski bum get any better than that!

This routine continued for about a month: skiing, dishwashing, eating, and generally having a great time. Then one day my life changed forever again. I came to work and the chef asked me if I wanted to be his assistant cook. That's the second in restaurant lingo. Something had happened to his second cook. He seemed to just disappear, something I've discovered over the years happens all the time in restaurants. I accepted the job. Why not? I liked it there. The job was not that complicated: learn to set up the salad bar. That was easy: half of the salad bar came out of cans. Keep it stocked during the night. Keep the baked potatoes and rice coming, and keep the chef happy. Kenny was moved into the bread station and was learning how to make great bread. He also handled the dessert station. We were both moving up in the world.

Kenny and I had a pact. Never give up. Always go for it no matter how busy we got. Don't get behind. That is curtains in a busy restaurant kitchen. It was fun and a little crazy and we enjoyed it. For some reason we liked chaos and thrived in it.

I think the owner kind of liked us. He was very conservative and we were very different, with our longish hair, shorts, hiking boots, and going-for-it attitude. We did a great job and he gave us the run of the place, though he always seemed slightly mystified about these two young longhairs spreading their fun mischief through his lodge.

Midway through the winter, on the chef's weekly day off, he wanted to go on a winter camping trip. He borrowed camping gear from most of the crew. I lent him my Coleman stove. Kenny lent him his sleeping bag. Everything seemed normal as he left for his winter adventure. We never saw him again.

When I came to work as I normally did to assume my second chef duties, I rudely discovered that there was no chef and that I would assume his duties immediately, with Kenny as my second. Now you have to understand that I was a young guy, was recently the dishwasher, had been assisting the chef with the low-level duties of the second for a short time, and we were in the middle of a very busy Aspen winter. But Kenny and I didn't care. Let's just go for it, we said. So that's what we did. Ignorance is truly bliss.

The first thing I set out to do was to create the nightly dinner special. I always watched the chef very closely so I had some idea of what to do. Now I'm not going to go into detail here about what I made. Suffice it to say that in the 1960s there were certain dishes that almost all ski area restaurants served. Somehow I knew that. So I made one of them. Having never made a special of any kind before, I just made it up. My own version of Chicken ala Orange. I don't remember what I served with it, but I did it.

Dan Weigner was very nervous that night as you would imagine. His chef had disappeared and two young man-children were running his kitchen. We did not look, act, or dress like chefs. But what we had going for us was that we really cared about doing a great job and serving great food. It was a challenge. Like standing at the top of a great and scary ski run and knowing you're going to give it your all going down and have a damn fine time doing it. That was our mentality. It was exhilarating.

Kenny and I cooked about 175 dinners that night. We got in that wild rhythm and plowed right through. I call it a controlled free fall. When we were finished cooking, Dan Weigner came back to the kitchen to visit with us. In his always restrained way he told me that the Chicken ala Orange was the best dinner special they had ever served at the Pomegranate Inn.

Over the next few years in Aspen, good jobs just seemed to come to me. It was a perfect training ground, better than any cooking school that existed in those days.

My first job after the Pomegranate was at a new French restaurant called Le Cheminee, owned by the elegant Frenchman Phillip Menu and his wife, Susan. They were very caring and graceful and they genuinely cared for me. But his French chef and glaring wife who had just come over from France hated my guts and made work a nightmare. I left after a short time because I didn't like having a constant stomachache over the chef's bad nature. But I did learn from him. I kept my eyes open.

The day I left Le Cheminee I got a job as a prep person at Aspen's most famous restaurant. It was The Copper Kettle owned by the great Sarah Armstrong and her husband, Army. They had been in the foreign service for years all over the world and brought a love of the world's foods to The Copper Kettle. They had a completely new menu every night and served about 300 people a night. You learn a lot in a place like that. Sarah's restaurant was her castle, and her generosity, loving spirit, and emphasis on quality ingredients made The Copper Kettle a great success and had a profound effect on the people she came in contact with. I will never forget her.

Andre's restaurant was my last stop in Aspen. The chef was the amazing David Batterson. He was a great chef, but he was much more than that. He was a great teacher of life. He was a man of many layers, moods, and complexities. David was like an older brother to me. He was always teaching me something, very little of which had anything to do with cooking.

Andre Ullrich was a true European. Highly educated, he spoke five languages and was very kind and generous. But you didn't want to be on his bad side. Andre's restaurant was wild and crazy. The employees were mostly outlaws in the spiritual sense of the word

who worked very hard and played even harder. It was a place in time that probably doesn't exist anymore. The world has become too conservative for such a wild band of gypsies.

I admired Andre very much for the long road he had traveled from Poland to Aspen and all the stops in between, and for the success he had. He was a man who would never give in or give up. Andre was very physical and loved to wrestle. One night in the restaurant kitchen Andre, as was his bent from time to time, got into a friendly sparring match with our waiter Don Lemos, noted private ski instructor, local Romeo, and a man not likely to back down from a challenge. As the fun progressed to something more serious, neither man would give up and the kitchen became total chaos. Now keep in mind we are in the middle of a busy night and here is our owner and a waiter groveling around on the floor, each half-serious about beating the tar out of the other one. Finally enough was enough, and it took half the staff to separate the sweaty, half-laughing, half-angry brawlers. With peace restored, the combatants cleaned themselves up and we all went back to work. And, as always with Andre, all was forgiven a short time later with no grudge held.

The last word I heard of Andre, he was moving to Katmandu to follow the spiritual life, his wrestling days behind him. The restaurant life will do that to a person.

I didn't learn cooking in any conventional way. I learned it because I loved doing it. It found me somehow on that night in the winter of 1969 at the Pomegranate Inn and because of what Dan Weigner said to me, lit the fuse of a life in cooking that continues today at Vintage, our unique, untamed little restaurant here in Ketchum, Idaho, Sun Valley, USA.

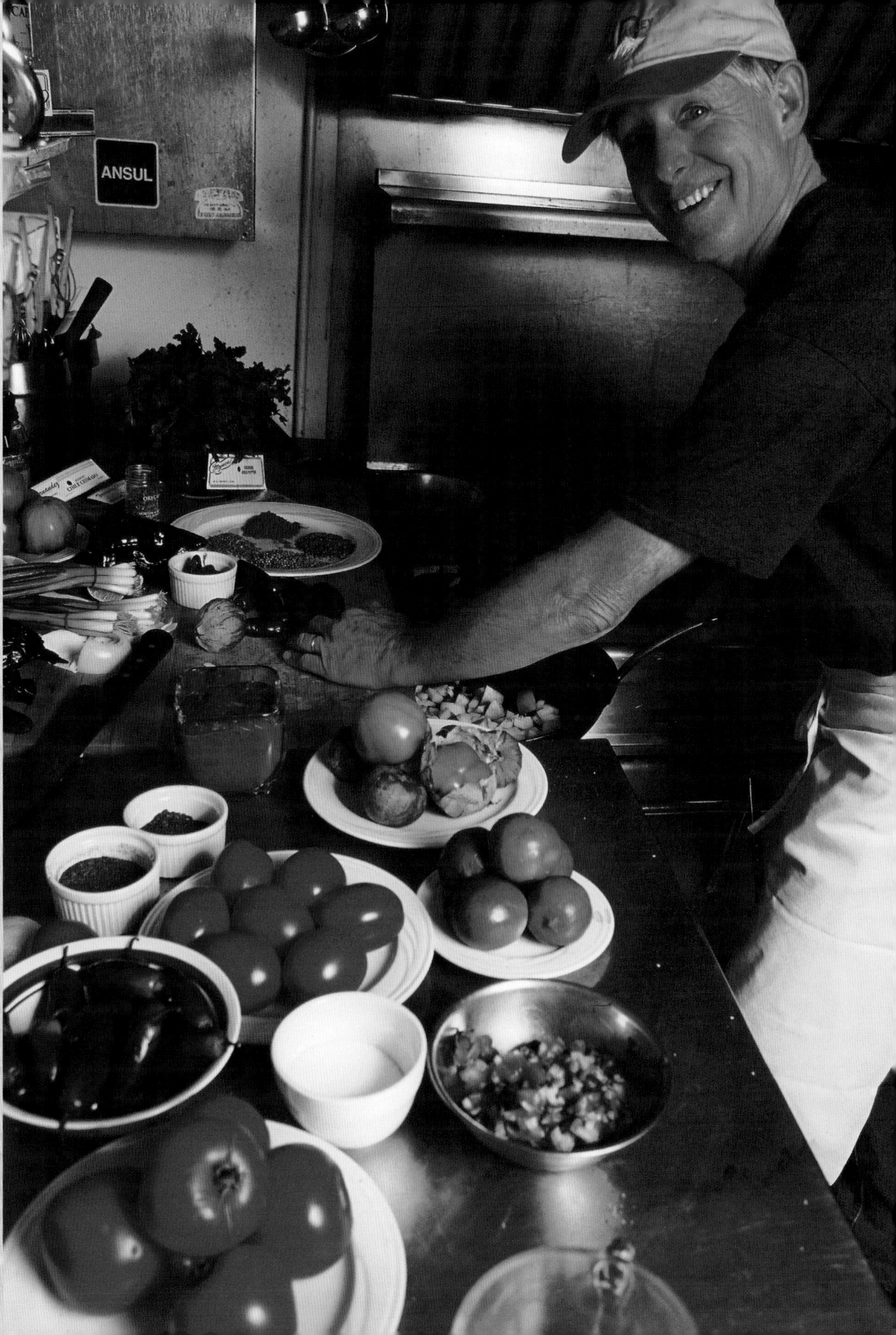
ANSUL

VINTAGE
style

■■■■

Vintage is a micro-wild area in the middle of a modern mountain town. It sprang up like a wild mushroom on an ancient tree trunk. My wife, Sheila, and I are the gardeners who twenty years ago planted the seeds and the trees that are Vintage today.

You just come upon Vintage. There is a sense of wonder and simplicity, an ageless quality in its walls and garden. You walk through the threshold and leave the modern world behind. It's a place that belongs to itself.

I like the idea of freedom, authenticity, wildness, and a sense of the primitive. I get excited by the energy and sense of fun when you don't know what to expect. I like the anticipation that you will be surprised and delighted. I like the edginess and the sense of the extreme that you feel in the high country that makes a community come closer together. And though our mountains are being airbrushed and manicured and refined by development, the mystery of nature, the wild energy that produces intense beauty, the constantly changing, always surprising, and slightly dangerous power of the mountains still remain. These are the qualities that I strive to bring alive at Vintage.

At Vintage we don't overwork or overstylize our food or our atmosphere. We are naturally elegant, rustic, warm, and friendly. We do as little handling of the food as possible. We let the natural beauty and intrinsic value of the ingredients tell us what to do. We let gravity do some of the work. We let the hidden nature of the mountains play a part. The inner burst of energy is important. We work with the way nature changes every day and we let that energy run through us.

On a dark and stormy day, the kind of day I love the most, I probably cook with a different feel than on one of our perfect, sunny and pristine, Idaho high-desert days. Comfort food,

like our Cream of Mushroom and Fresh Herb Soup, Old-Fashioned Crispy-Skin Roast Duckling with Wild Rice Toasted Pecan Pilaf and Baked Apple Brandy Compote, and Chocolate Chunk Bread Pudding with Steamy Whiskey Sabayon Sauce are what I might cook on that dark and stormy day. It would be fun.

When it's sunny and clear as crystal I might serve lightly curried Avocado Gazpacho, Fresh Mahimahi, South Pacific Style, with a beach-stand Mango Salsa, Crispy Noodles, and Golden Plum, Hoisin, Sesame Drizzle. For dessert I'd serve a fresh fruit strudel with a scoop of my Mountain Decadence Ice Cream. Or Mountain Decadence Ice Cream with Bachelors' Berries. Now that feels right on a crystalline blue-sky day with a Maxfield Parrish sunset.

I like to cook what I feel, and I arrange the menus so I can do that. Vintage is not a machine-driven restaurant. We don't have the fanciest equipment. We have very little space. We are handmade in every sense of the word. But our boundaries are our gifts. Our limitations make us unique. We have imagination and not too many preconceived notions. There is a wide expanse in that. The elements make cooking fun and interesting, and the idea is to capture the flavor and create a little magic. That's Vintage Style and here are a few of those elements and basic recipes that make it come alive.

■ ■ ■ ■

Vintage Spice Mix

This spice mix and the *Peppery Orange Aioli* to follow are the true spirits of Vintage. They run through all of my cooking, their origins from around the world coming out in our food. I use this spice mix in roasting meats, in BBQ spice rubs, and BBQ sauces. Sprinkle a little or a lot on chicken breasts and then grill or fry them. Sprinkle some on a steak or put a little in a slow-cooked stew. It's great stuff to have around to add distinction to your cooking.

Makes 1 cup dry spice mix

2	tablespoons good quality mild New Mexico chile powder
1	tablespoon Spanish paprika
1	tablespoon fresh ground black pepper
1	tablespoon kosher salt
1	tablespoon ground toasted cumin seed
1	tablespoon whole fennel seed
1	tablespoon curry powder
1	tablespoon dry whole-leaf thyme
1	tablespoon cayenne pepper
1	tablespoon onion powder
1	tablespoon granulated garlic

Mix all the ingredients together and store in a tightly covered container. It's at its best for 30 days.

Peppery Orange Aioli

In southern France, aioli is not a delicious condiment; it is a state of mind. It is a relaxed attitude toward life. It is understanding what is important. It is slowing down on a hot afternoon under shady trees at a table, eating the grand aioli. It is platters of vegetables to be eaten with aioli alongside glasses of cool wine. It is visiting with friends and loved ones and sharing the time. Slowing down the time and appreciating life. That attitude makes me feel better and that is why I make *Peppery Orange Aioli*. This is definitely my version of aioli. A French person might cringe. But let's take the freedom to start our own traditions. I'm glad the French are there to learn from.

Makes 1½ cups

1	large fresh egg yolk
1	tablespoon French Dijon mustard
5	medium-size cloves garlic, smashed
¼	teaspoon fresh ground black pepper
	Pinch kosher salt
1½	tablespoons chopped parsley
1½	teaspoons finely grated orange zest
½	teaspoon finely grated lemon zest
	Juice of ½ lemon
1	cup plus 2 tablespoons light olive oil
1	tablespoon warm water

To make the aioli, put the first nine ingredients in a food processor. While running the food processor, drizzle the oil in slowly so the mixture absorbs the oil and forms the aioli. It's like a mayonnaise in structure. When all of the oil is incorporated, add the warm water. Store the aioli in a jar or small bowl and cover tightly.

This aioli goes great with fish or chicken. Use it anywhere you would use mayonnaise. A great trick using aioli is to rub a little on fillets of fish you are going to grill and they won't stick to the grill. It will also add a nice flavor.

VINTAGE GARLIC BUTTER

Call me old-fashioned, but I still use garlic butter. It started years ago when snails were all the rage. I grew out of that one, but today I always have garlic butter around. And as you will see in the book, it is used in two dishes that are the real expression of Vintage style. Besides, do we ever get tired of a good garlic bread? I don't think so.

Makes 3 cups

1	pound unsalted butter
30	medium-size cloves garlic
3	green onions, chopped
⅓	cup chopped parsley

Cut butter into quarters and let it come to room temperature in a mixing bowl. Put garlic, green onions, and parsley in a food processor and pulse until they are chopped. Add the chopped ingredients to the butter and thoroughly blend. Store the garlic butter in the refrigerator in a container with a tight-fitting lid. Will store for up to 10 days.

BRAISED GARLIC CLOVES IN OLIVE OIL

This is a condiment I always have on hand because I can use it in so many different ways. Use the garlic oil in salad dressing, to brush on grilled bread, to make croutons, or to sauté fish and chicken breasts. Use the braised garlic with lemony white beans, in garlic chowder, to serve as a condiment with steak or lamb, in garlic smashed potatoes, or to spread on warmed bread. If you like garlic, you'll love Braised Garlic Cloves.

Makes 1¼ cups

1	cup light olive oil
20	cloves garlic, peeled

Put olive oil and garlic cloves in a small saucepan and heat the oil over low heat to a very slow simmer. Cook for about 20 minutes, or until the garlic is nice and soft. If garlic browns, your heat is too high—turn it down. Cool the mixture and store in a bowl or jar with a tight-fitting lid. This stores for 10 days in the refrigerator.

SOUTHERN DARK BEER AND BROWN SUGAR MARINADE

This is a great marinade for pork—ribs especially. Make a mixed grill with pork ribs, halves of Cornish game hens, and spicy sausage. Marinate the meats overnight, smoke them on hickory in a cold smoker, then roast them in the oven or on the BBQ. Serve them with caramelized yams and Spicy New Orleans Slaw (see page 77) and you will be in heaven.

Makes about 2 cups

1	12-ounce bottle of dark beer (I like Moose Drool—what could be better in this marinade?)
4	tablespoons dark brown sugar
2	teaspoons Vintage Spice Mix (see page 27)

Mix the ingredients together in a bowl and use immediately.

VINTAGE BASIC ASIAN MARINADE

This is sort of my marinade for everything. I use it on meats I'm going to smoke in the cold smoker. The sweet and hot in the marinade has a magic chemistry with smoke. I use it to marinate fish, lamb, pork, or chicken that I'm going to grill. (Again it has good chemistry, but don't marinate fish very long because it is potent.) Vintage Basic Asian Marinade is also a great base to make other marinades and Asian drizzles.

Makes 2¾ cups

2	cups soy sauce (find one that is not too salty)
12	tablespoons brown sugar
1	tablespoon plus 1 teaspoon coarse ground black pepper
2	teaspoons whole fennel seeds
10	cloves garlic, mashed and diced
3	tablespoons fresh grated ginger

Mix all the ingredients together in a bowl. This marinade is very potent so it will absorb quickly into meat. If marinating fish, just put it in and out. For chicken breasts and pork chops, marinate 5 minutes. For butterflied leg of lamb, 15 minutes. Or in and out for anything to which you want to add a little extra flavor. This stores for 10 days in the refrigerator.

ASIAN SMOKING MARINADE

This is a more complex marinade. You can use it in the same way you use the Vintage Basic Asian Marinade.

Makes 2 cups

- 1 cup Vintage Basic Asian Marinade (see page 29)
- ½ cup dry sherry
- 1 teaspoon ground cinnamon
- 1 teaspoon ground star anise
- ½ teaspoon ground cloves
- ½ cup strong Asian tea

Mix all the ingredients together in a bowl. This marinade is especially good with chicken or duck, and you can marinate the meats longer than with Vintage Basic Asian Marinade since this version is more subtle because of the sherry and the tea. Use this marinade on meats you are going to cold smoke. I use this marinade with fish that I'm going to sear on the BBQ or charbroiler and then serve Chinese sesame BBQ style.

CAULIFLOWER AND OLIVE SALAD

These crispy and tangy roasted vegetables make a great accompaniment for your favorite entrée. It's also fun to vary the vegetable combinations. Try the dish with artichoke wedges, roasted red bell pepper strips, potato wedges, and broccoli florets.

Makes 4 servings

- 2 cups cauliflower florets
- 2 tablespoons unsalted butter
- 12 pitted kalamata olives
- 1 tablespoon thinly sliced fresh basil
- 1½ tablespoons saltine cracker crumbs
- 1 tablespoon freshly squeezed lemon juice

Preheat oven to 425 degrees F. Steam the cauliflower florets until they are just fork-tender, about 4 minutes. Don't overcook them! Plunge cauliflower into cold water so it stops cooking. Drain on a paper towel.

Melt the butter in a 10-inch, ovenproof sauté pan. First add cauliflower florets, then the olives and basil; toss with the hot butter. Now sprinkle saltine cracker crumbs over the top and toss again so the crumbs coat the vegetables. Sprinkle the dish with the lemon juice. Put the sauté pan in the oven for about 4 to 5 minutes, or until the cracker crumbs are crispy and the dish is hot. Serve immediately.

THE ART OF COLD SMOKING

About twenty years ago I got a true hankering to serve smoked meat dishes. I could buy smoked meats, but I wanted to do it myself. My restaurant kitchen at my old Soupcon, now Vintage, did not have the space to add a smoker, and I didn't really want to go whole hog and become a smokehouse. I just wanted to explore another technique of cooking. I needed another solution and one day by chance I found one. It came in the form of The Little Chief Smoker that I discovered in our local hardware store. Of course I bought one immediately. It was under 100 bucks. Very reasonable. I have not lived without one since.

The Little Chief Smoker is used for cold smoking. The smoker produces smoke but very little heat. It flavors meat, fish, or even vegetables, with real wood smoke. You can also influence the flavor by marinating the meat first before smoking it. This freed me in a very simple way to expand the whole range of my cooking. Now, hardly a day goes by when I don't have a smoked dish on the menu.

It's a fun technique because you can use different varieties of wood chips, like apple wood, hickory, cherry, or mesquite to get different flavors and intensities of smoke into your food. You can play with it to find out what combination of wood goes well with different marinades and different meats. It's truly an inexpensive way to make your cooking more interesting and delicious. I find that what makes life interesting is learning something new all the time. With the smoker I learned to infuse the meat with the flavor of the smoke and then in the evening I could roast, grill, or sauté the meat to perfection and have a wonderful smoky flavor. The art of life is figuring out your way of doing something. If you love good eating, and I suspect that you do, try out cold smoking. It will be something you really look forward to doing.

luscious starters

■■■■

Starters are for me a little trip somewhere. A postcard, an experience all its own. Starters should be surprising, unexpected, eclectic. Little mouthfuls of explosive taste. Something I brought home from France by way of Carmel, New York City, the Sea of Cortez, New Orleans. I don't really care where. Just start me on a trip somewhere. I'll willingly go.

I like starters to be spicy and bright. I want the starter to wake up your taste buds, to stimulate your appetite, to get you excited about the coming meal.

I also enjoy starters that you can have with a salad and some good bread—then you have a full meal. It's a casual bistro style and a fun way to eat. You can eat that way at Vintage. Lots of our guests do. Have a soup or salad, Spicy Cajun Oysters or a Rock Shrimp Tamale, then some Mountain Decadence Ice Cream and a cup of coffee (after the wine, of course). That makes a great meal. Leave the heavy hitters for another time.

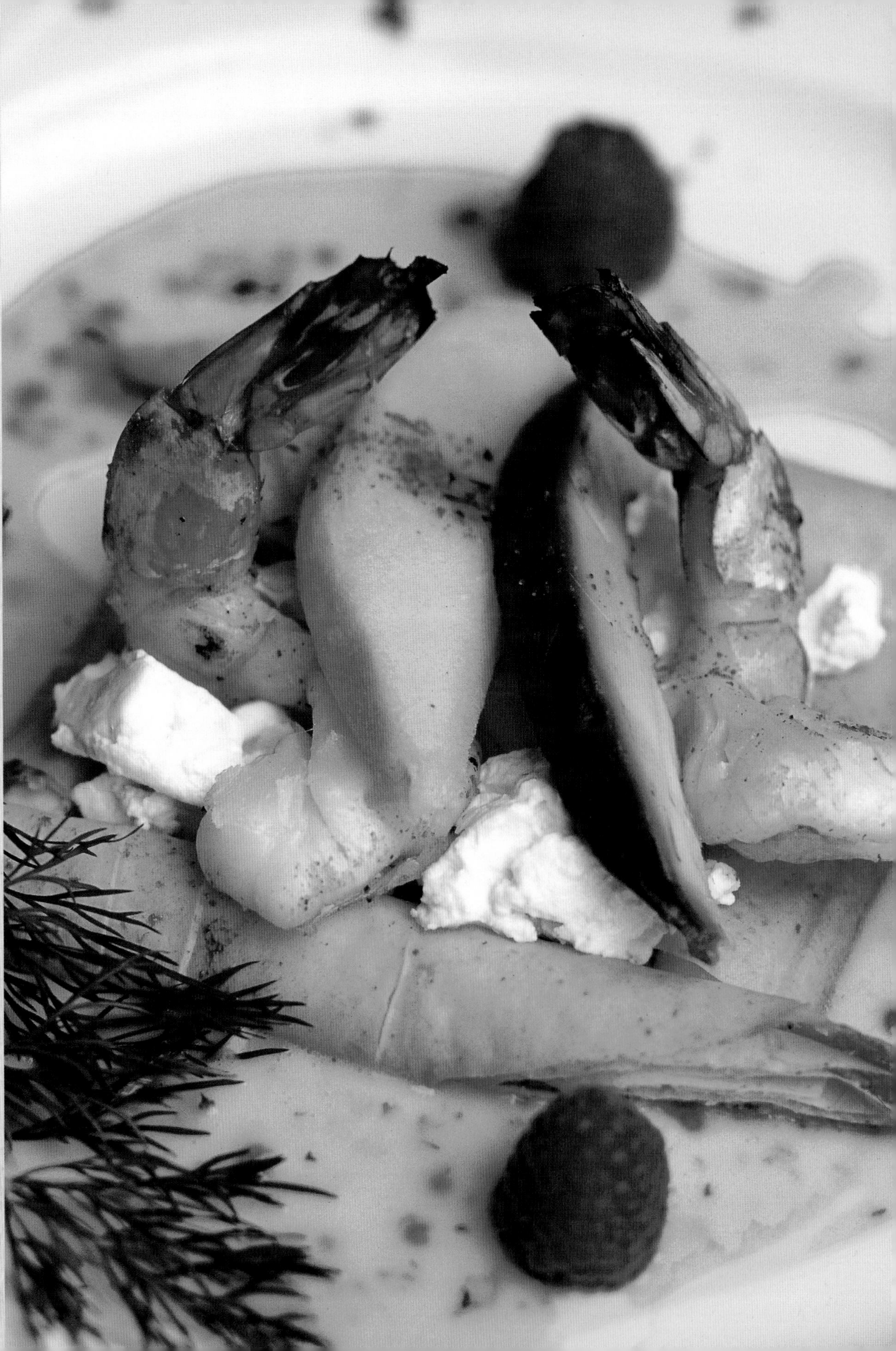

PRAWN AND GOAT CHEESE TART

This dish is a beautiful little beginning to a meal. It is from France with a detour through Carmel, California. My good friend Chef Craig Ling owned Restaurant Crème Carmel in Carmel back in the 1980s. He was doing a Southwestern version of this dish back then. I loved it. Sheila and I had gone to France and upon returning I realized a French version of Prawn and Goat Cheese Tart was in order. It would be a nice variation on Craig's work. It was a huge hit. So with full credit to Craig Ling for the idea, here is my version of this delightful dish. This dish has a number of elements to make before you put it together, so here they are in the order you should make them.

Makes 4 servings

For the Tart Shells:

- 4 sheets (12 x 17 inches each) phyllo dough
- ½ cup unsalted butter, melted
- ½ teaspoon dry whole-leaf thyme
- 1 cup finely ground saltine cracker crumbs

For the White Butter Sauce:

- ½ cup fruity white wine (I like an Alsatian Pinot Blanc)
- Juice from ½ lemon
- Pinch saffron threads
- ½ teaspoon pink peppercorns
- 2 tablespoons heavy cream
- ½ cup unsalted butter, cut in small pieces and frozen
- ½ teaspoon finely chopped parsley

For the tart:

- 16 teaspoons goat cheese
- 8 lightly steamed 16/20 size prawns
- 8 slices fresh mango, about ¼ inch thick
- 4 slices avocado, ¼ inch thick
- Sprinkling of Vintage Spice Mix (see page 27)
- Juice from ½ lemon
- 16 fresh raspberries for garnish
- Fresh dill for garnish

To make the tart shells, preheat oven to 375 degrees F. Lay out 2 phyllo sheets onto a wooden cutting board (see photos on page 36). Cut them in half on the short side. Now you have 2 sets of phyllo sheets that are 12 x 8½ inches. Brush top sheet of each set with melted butter using a pastry brush. In a small bowl, mix thyme with saltine cracker crumbs and lightly sprinkle over phyllo sheets. Roll up the edges of the phyllo sheets to form a 4- x 5-inch tart shell. Follow the same procedure with remaining phyllo and you will have 4 tart shells. Put the tart shells on a lightly oiled baking sheet and bake about 6 minutes or until golden brown. Remove from oven and let cool. You can make the tart shells several hours to a day ahead of time. The tart shells are flaky so keep them in a safe place.

To make the white butter sauce, add white wine, lemon juice, saffron, and pink peppercorns to a small saucepan; bring to a simmer and reduce by two-thirds. Add cream and simmer until the sauce reduces by one-third. Turn off heat. Whisk in the first piece of frozen butter, then the next piece of frozen butter. Now turn the heat back on very low and whisk in remaining butter until it is all fully incorporated. Sprinkle in parsley. Set the white butter sauce aside in a warm place. You are now ready to assemble the tarts.

Preheat oven to 475 degrees F. Assemble the tarts by placing each tart shell on an ovenproof plate. Put a teaspoon of goat cheese in each corner of each tart shell. Place 2 prawns in the middle of each tart shell, tail up. Now place 2 slices of mango and 1 slice of avocado over the prawns with the avocado in the middle. Sprinkle prawns with the slightest pinch of Vintage Spice Mix. Squeeze a little lemon juice over each tart. Bake tarts in the oven for about 5 minutes. They should be hot, the cheese warmed through but not overcooked. To serve, ladle a pool of the white butter sauce onto the center of four warm plates. Place 1 tart just off center on each plate. Place 4 fresh raspberries around each plate and a sprig of fresh dill to garnish. Serve immediately.

SPICY CAJUN OYSTERS

Spicy Cajun Oysters are without a doubt our most requested dish. Guests have double orders for dinner. A few have even ordered it for dessert. I cannot go to the restaurant and not serve it. Our guests demand it. And I love to make it. This dish is my homage to New Orleans. It's what I imagine and what I feel about the Cajun way of eating. It's hot and spicy, yet refreshing. You cannot stop eating it—you'll be dipping bread in the broth until every drop is gone! Close your eyes. You are now deep in the heart of Cajun country.

Makes 2 servings

- 8 medium-size fresh shucked oysters
- 1 tablespoon Vintage Spice Mix (see page 27)
- 2 tablespoons plus 1 teaspoon Vintage Garlic Butter (see page 28)
- ⅓ cup fish or chicken stock (store-bought is fine)
- 1 tablespoon freshly squeezed lemon juice
- 2 tablespoons Peppery Orange Aioli (see page 27)
- 2 tablespoons Vintage Pico de Gallo (see page 110)
- 1 green onion, thinly sliced diagonally

Put oysters on a plate and sprinkle with Vintage Spice Mix. Melt 2 tablespoons Vintage Garlic Butter in a 10-inch sauté pan, being careful not to burn the garlic. When the butter is hot, slide the oysters into the sauté pan and cook for about 1½ minutes; then turn them over and cook on the other side for 1½ minutes. Remove oysters immediately to two awaiting bowls.

To the pan the oysters were cooked in, add stock, lemon juice, and 1 teaspoon Vintage Garlic Butter. Cook just until butter melts and then pour sauce evenly over the two bowls of oysters. Garnish each bowl with a tablespoon dollop of Peppery Orange Aioli and a tablespoon dollop of Pico de Gallo. Sprinkle each dish with thinly sliced green onions. Serve with lots of warm bread on the side for dipping.

LOS BARILLES ROCK SHRIMP SWEET CORN TAMALES

These are my style of tamale. I make sweet corn tamales with no additional filling. I steam them. When they are served, I cut them open, give them a little squeeze, and then pour in my freshly made filling. In this case it is rock shrimp. I know that tamales are a holiday tradition in Mexico, but I serve them year-round. Sometimes I make the tamale masa and mix it two-thirds masa to one-third mashed baked yam. I serve it with roasted and sliced lamb rack or seared flatiron steak with a spice mix rub, grilled and thinly sliced. Try it—it's great. The tamale alone is worth it. We named this version after a little windy town on the Sea of Cortez because it's such a peaceful place to go lie on the beach for a few days, eat street stand shrimp tacos with great condiments, and let the kids run free.

Makes 12 tamales

For the Tamales:

15 dry cornhusks

2½ cups Mexican masa mix specifically for tamales (you can find this in the Mexican section of most supermarkets)

1½ teaspoons baking powder

½ teaspoon kosher salt

Fresh-cut corn from 2 to 3 ears corn or 1-pound package frozen sweet corn, thawed

1 tablespoon sugar

1 teaspoon fresh ground toasted cumin seed

1½ teaspoons mild New Mexico chile powder

⅓ cup freshly snipped cilantro

⅔ cup salad oil

½ cup hot water

For the Filling:

5 ounces rock shrimp

Vintage Spice Mix (see page 27)

2 tablespoons plus 1 teaspoon Vintage Garlic Butter (see page 28)

½ cup fish or chicken stock

1 lemon

Vintage Pico de Gallo (see page 110)

Peppery Orange Aioli (see page 27)

1 green onion, thinly sliced diagonally

Put cornhusks in a pot of boiling water and let them simmer for about 15 minutes. This will rehydrate the husks and make them pliable so you can wrap up the tamales. After husks have become pliable, take them out of the water to drain and cool. Tear 2 or 3 of the husks into ¼-inch strips to use as ties for the tamales.

In a bowl, mix together all remaining ingredients for the tamales. The masa should come together and hold its form, but shouldn't be too wet. You want it crumbly, but able to come together when you form the tamale. If it is too dry, add a little more hot water.

Now you can wrap up the tamales in the cornhusks. Take a small handful of masa in your hand and form a cylinder about 1 inch wide and 3 inches long. Place this on the center edge of a husk and roll up the husk. Twist each end of the husk closed and tie with a husk strip. Repeat until you have about 12 tamales. You can make them smaller or larger if you want. Tamales will keep at this point for a day or two in the refrigerator if you want to make them ahead of time. They also freeze great!

When you are ready to cook the tamales, lightly boil water in a pot with a steamer basket. Put in as many tamales as you are going to serve, cover the pot, and steam for 30 to 40 minutes. When the tamales are ready, prepare the rock shrimp.

Place shrimp in a bowl and sprinkle a little Vintage Spice Mix over them. Use a heavy sprinkling for really spicy shrimp, less for milder. Melt 2 tablespoons Vintage Garlic Butter in a 6-inch sauté pan over medium heat. Add rock shrimp and cook for about 2 minutes. Add stock, a big squirt of lemon juice, and about 1 teaspoon more of the garlic butter. Bring up to high heat and cook for 1 minute. The mixture should be simmering and the rock shrimp just done. Put 1 steaming tamale into each serving bowl. With a knife, make a cut across the length of the tamale and, using your hands, give a little squeeze to each end of the tamale to open it up. Spoon equal parts of the rock shrimp and the broth into each tamale. Use all of the broth. There should be a nice pool of broth in each bowl. Now garnish the dish with a tablespoon of Vintage Pico de Gallo and a dollop of Peppery Orange Aioli. Sprinkle with some sliced green onion and serve.

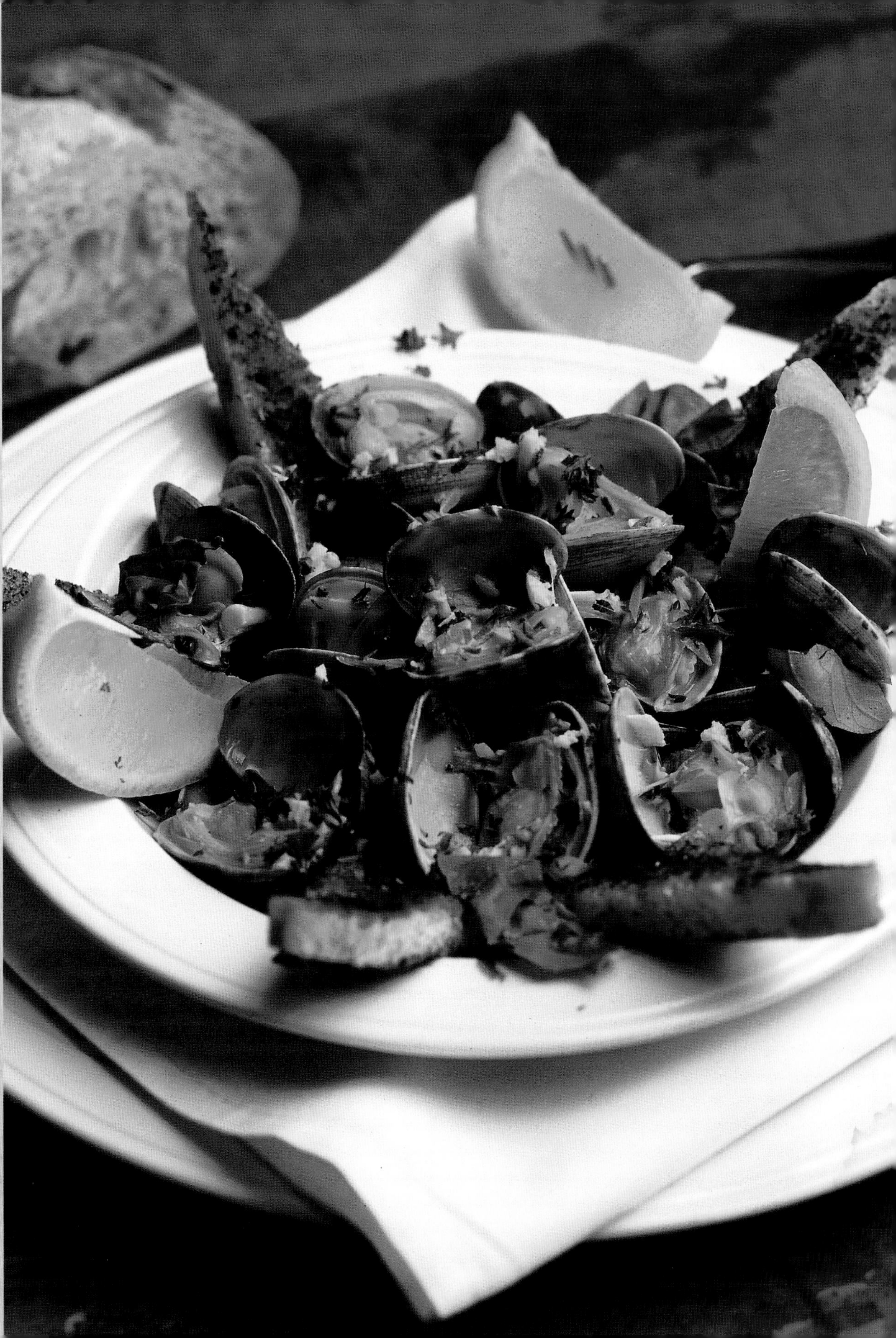

Olympic Peninsula Steamer Clams

When you need a dish that is fast to make, fresh, and delicious, look no further than these steamer clams. The prep time is a few minutes. The cooking time is a few minutes. They will get you off the hook when you don't have much time. And a chef never has enough time, so they are perfect.

Makes 2 servings

For the Croutons:

Baguette

Olive oil

New Mexico chile powder

For the Clams:

24   fresh steamer clams, rinsed of any grit or sand and covered with a damp towel

3   tablespoons Vintage Garlic Butter (see page 28)

Juice of ½ lemon

2   tablespoons dry white wine

2   tablespoons snipped mixed fresh herbs such as basil, parsley, and celery leaf

8   lemon wedges

To make the croutons, make 8 V-shaped ¼-inch-thick slices from a good baguette. Brush with some olive oil, sprinkle lightly with some good New Mexico chile powder, and sear in a hot pan or on a broiler or BBQ. Set aside.

To cook the clams, place them in a 12-inch sauté pan and rinse them off really well under cold running water. Drain the water off and add Vintage Garlic Butter in small pieces, lemon juice, and white wine to the pan. Cook over high heat with another 12-inch sauté pan inverted over the top to form a lid. The garlic butter will melt, the juices will begin to steam, and the clams will start to open up and release their briny juices into the broth. As soon as the clams open up, stop cooking them. If some are partially opened that's okay. They are done. (One of my pet peeves with clams is that most people overcook them. So don't. You'll see that these are perfect when you try them.) If any clams don't open, discard them. Divide clams into 2 serving bowls. Pour the broth over the top and sprinkle with the fresh herbs. Place red chile croutons around the bowl and serve with lemon wedges. The broth is delicious so serve with extra baguette slices or other good bread for dipping.

LIGHTLY SMOKED WILD KING SALMON PÂTÉ

This pâté is a great way to begin a meal any time of year. I get my smoked salmon from a local smoker, Tom Hickey, who sends his Sun Valley Smoked Salmon to high-quality food shops all over the country. His smoked salmon is light and moist and is the perfect salmon for this pâté. I put a thin frosting of sour cream mixed with a few drops of balsamic vinegar over each pâté and then serve it with warm grilled crostini brushed with a little garlicky olive oil.

Makes 6 to 7 servings

For the Pâté:

12	ounces moist wood-smoked salmon
1	cup chive-and-onion cream cheese
1	tablespoon Dijon mustard
1	tablespoon drained capers plus extra for serving
1	tablespoon chopped parsley
2	teaspoons freshly snipped dill
	Juice of ¾ medium-size lemon
3	tablespoons sour cream
⅛	teaspoon fresh ground black pepper
⅛	teaspoon kosher salt
	Red bell pepper for serving
	Fresh dill for serving

For the Frosting:

½	cup sour cream
¾	teaspoon balsamic vinegar

To make the pâté, put all the ingredients except the red bell pepper and fresh dill into a food processor and pulse until the mixture is thoroughly blended. It should have a nice firm but creamy body that will spread nicely on crostini, crackers, or warm baguette. Spoon the pâté into six or seven 5-ounce pâté crocks to about ¼ inch from the top of the crock.

To make the frosting, mix the sour cream and balsamic vinegar in a small bowl until thoroughly blended. Apply an even, thin layer of the frosting to the top of each pâté crock.

To serve, sprinkle each pâté with 5 or 6 capers, two very thin slices of red bell pepper, and a sprig of fresh dill. Surround the crocks with grilled crostini or warm bread and dig in.

SMOKED VALENTINA CHICKEN WINGS

We discovered Valentina hot sauce at street stand taco bars along the Sea of Cortez in Mexico. This is my take on buffalo wings but from south-of-the-border. Cold smoking the wings adds multiple layers of flavor. The wings are smoky and they are hot and spicy. And the Hair-of-the-Dog Dipping Sauce will have you begging for mercy while coming back for more!

Makes 4 servings

2	pounds chicken wings, washed and patted dry
½	cup Vintage Basic Asian Marinade (see page 29)
2	tablespoons Vintage Spice Mix (see page 27)
½	cup Valentina Mexican hot sauce (you can find this at most supermarkets)
4	jalapeño peppers, pan-seared
	Oil
4	green onions, trimmed and grilled
	Hair-of-the-Dog Dipping Sauce (see page 111)

On a cutting board, cut off the tip joint of each chicken wing, and then cut the wing through the remaining joint so you have two pieces per wing. Prepare all the wings this way. Put them in a bowl and toss them in the Vintage Basic Asian Marinade. Pour off excess marinade. Next toss the wings with the Vintage Spice Mix. Now they are ready to smoke.

Prepare the Little Chief Smoker (see page 31). I like to use hickory wood chips for smoking the wings. Put wings in the smoker and smoke for about 30 minutes. They won't cook in the smoker but will be infused with a delicious smoky flavor. Remove wings from smoker. Place on a baking sheet and roast in the oven for about 20 minutes at 400 degrees F. Remove from oven and place in a bowl; toss immediately with Valentina Mexican hot sauce.

To pan sear the jalapeños, put a thin coating of vegetable oil in a sauté pan over medium heat. When oil is hot, add jalapeños and cook them on all sides for a total of about 7 minutes. The skin will blister and the pepper will soften up. (Jalapeños are great pickled with a little oil and vinegar and a pinch of salt.) To grill the green onions, brush very lightly with oil and cook on a broiler for 1 minute per side.

Serve hot wings on a platter with a bowl of the Hair-of-the-Dog Dipping Sauce, pan-seared jalapeño peppers, and grilled green onions.

WILD MOUNTAIN WHITE PIZZAS

These pizzas are just plain fun to eat. They are stuffed with white Farmers Cheese mix, fresh herbs, and a brushing of olive oil. They are baked quickly in a very hot oven and then topped with salads, grilled meat, or roasted vegetables and drizzled with vinaigrettes or white truffle oil. The imagination is the only limitation. I've included four of my favorite toppings. Instead of making my own pizza crusts, which I don't have time to do anyway, I discovered these great pizza crusts at my local Atkinson's Market. They are Boboli Pizza Crusts. I use them for my pizzas and I recommend them. They are thick enough that they can be cut in half horizontally and stuffed with white cheese. We all need easy little secrets to get us through, and these crusts are one of those secrets. Besides they are really good. I use the 6-inch diameter pizza crusts for these pizzas.

Makes 4 pizza crusts

For the Crust:

4   Boboli 6-inch pizza crusts

For the Farmers Cheese:

½   cup cream cheese

4   ounces Montrachet goat cheese

¼   teaspoon fresh ground black pepper, (optional)

1   tablespoon diced fresh herbs like thyme, basil, or oregano

For the Fresh Basil Oil:

2   tablespoons thinly sliced fresh basil

¾   cup olive oil

To make the Farmers Cheese, soften the two cheeses to room temperature and then blend together in a bowl with the pepper and fresh snipped herbs, if using. Set aside.

To make the Fresh Basil Oil, in a separate bowl, mash the basil together with the olive oil. Set aside.

To assemble the pizzas, slice pizza crusts all the way through the center of the crust horizontally. With a pastry brush, lightly brush each interior half of the crust with a little basil oil. Spread 2 ounces Farmers Cheese evenly over the bottom half of each crust. Put the top half back on the bottom half. Brush a little of the basil oil on the pizza top. Preheat oven to 475 degrees F. Use one of the recipes that follow for baking and topping.

Bacon-Wrapped Grilled Fresh Spring Asparagus Pizza

Makes 1 pizza

1   Wild Mountain White Pizza (see page 45)

4   lightly steamed asparagus spears

2   partially cooked pieces smoked bacon

½   teaspoon white truffle oil

Wrap 2 asparagus spears with a slice of bacon and secure with a toothpick. Repeat. Put cheese-filled pizza crust in oven for 5 minutes. While pizza is cooking, grill bacon-wrapped asparagus spears on the charbroiler or put them in the oven with the pizza if you don't have a broiler. (You can also cook them both on your BBQ.) When 5 minutes are up, remove pizza from oven to a cutting board and slice into quarters. Remove asparagus from broiler and remove toothpicks. Place the 4 pizza slices on a serving plate. Top with the bacon-wrapped asparagus and drizzle with white truffle oil. Serve.

Grilled Chile-Lime Prawn Salad Pizza

Makes 1 pizza

1   Wild Mountain White Pizza (see page 45)

Grilled Chile-Lime Prawn Salad (see page 71)

Make the Grilled Chile-Lime Prawn Salad and finish the salad about the time you put the pizza in the oven. Cook cheese-filled pizza crust for 5 minutes and then remove from oven to a cutting board and slice into quarters. Place on a serving plate. Top with a healthy serving of the salad. Serve. The full recipe for the salad is enough to serve with four of the pizzas.

Another salad variation for topping cheese-filled pizza is using simple mixed greens with thin slices of sweet onion and a drizzle of Balsamic Vinaigrette (see page 61). Or try using a spoonful or two of Heirloom Tomato Salad (see page 65).

GRILLED MUSHROOMS AND BALSAMIC VINAIGRETTE DRIZZLE PIZZA

Makes 1 pizza

1	Wild Mountain White Pizza (see page 45)
¾	cup mixed mushrooms such as shiitake, morel, and chanterelle
1	tablespoon olive oil
1	¼-inch slice sweet onion
	Pinch each kosher salt and freshly ground black pepper
	Balsamic Vinaigrette (see page 61)
½	tablespoon each freshly snipped parsley and thyme

Put cheese-filled pizza in oven for 5 minutes. While it is cooking, toss mushrooms in olive oil and brush onion slice with a little olive oil. Sprinkle the mushrooms and onion slice with a pinch of salt and pepper; grill on the broiler for about 3 minutes. Remove from broiler and dice onion. Toss onion in a bowl with grilled mushrooms and a squirt of Balsamic Vinaigrette. Remove pizza from oven to a cutting board and slice into quarters. Put it on a serving plate and top with the grilled mushroom-and-onion mixture. Sprinkle with freshly snipped herbs and serve.

GRILLED SLICED SMOKED MUSCOVY DUCK BREAST PIZZA

Makes 1 pizza

1	Wild Mountain White Pizza (see page 45)
4	thin slices Smoked Muscovy Duck Breast (see page 127)
	White truffle oil

Put cheese-filled pizza crust in oven for 5 minutes. While it is cooking, warm smoked duck breast slices on the broiler or in a sauté pan for a few minutes. Remove pizza from oven to a cutting board and slice into quarters. Put it on a serving plate and arrange duck breast slices on the pizza slices. Drizzle with a little white truffle oil and serve. You can also try this pizza with good smoked ham slices in place of the duck breast. I also like to use very thin slices of prosciutto, letting the hot pizza warm the prosciutto.

Fresh Ahi Tuna Satay

Satay *is a Southeast Asian word meaning "skewered and grilled." This is sidewalk street stand food and a great way to start a meal. Fresh Ahi Tuna Satay are great little stimulators because they really perk up the appetite. They are great made with other fish, chicken, pork, lamb, or beef, too. They go well with a variety of marinades and dipping sauces, so they are really fun to play around with. Explore the world of satays and discover a whole new range of cooking. Serve this satay with a Jasmine Rice Cake, Pink Grapefruit and Jicama Slaw, and Asian Dipping Sauce.*

Makes 4 servings

For the Jasmine Rice Cakes:

3   cups water

1½ cups jasmine rice, uncooked

1   tablespoon unsalted butter

1   tablespoon sugar

    Pinch kosher salt

2   tablespoons diced green onion

1½ tablespoons seasoned rice wine vinegar

For the Pink Grapefruit and Jicama Slaw:

    Tropical Mango, Jicama, and Pineapple Slaw (see page 76)

½   pink grapefruit, cut into thin wedges

For the Asian Dipping Sauce:

1   cup Vintage Basic Asian Marinade (see page 29)

⅛   teaspoon red chile flakes

1   tablespoon thinly sliced green onion

2   teaspoons Thai fish sauce

1   tablespoon hoisin sauce

1   tablespoon Asian black vinegar or balsamic vinegar

Pinch ground star anise

For the Satays:

1   pound fresh sashimi-grade ahi tuna, cut in 1-ounce pieces

¼   cup Vintage Basic Asian Marinade (see page 29)

4   wooden 6-inch skewers

To make the Jasmine Rice Cakes, bring the water to a boil in a saucepan and add the rice, butter, sugar, and salt. Bring back to a boil and stir. Cover the pan and turn the heat down to a high simmer; cook for about 15 to 20 minutes until the water has been absorbed and the rice is tender but not overcooked. Fluff up the rice with a spoon and stir in the green onion and rice vinegar. Lightly oil an 8- x 8-inch Pyrex cake pan, pour the rice into it, and spread evenly. Cover with a sheet of plastic wrap, leaving a little room along the edges for the heat to escape. Refrigerate to cool thoroughly.

Make the Tropical Mango, Jicama, and Pineapple Slaw, but replace the mango with pink grapefruit. Set aside.

In a small bowl, mix together all the ingredients for the Asian Dipping Sauce; cover and set aside.

To make the satays, put the ahi pieces in a mixing bowl and toss them with the marinade. Thread 4 pieces of ahi onto each skewer, placing them ¼ inch apart.

To finish the dish, set out four serving plates. Cut the jasmine rice into 1½-inch square cakes and place one rice cake on each plate. Place a bed of Pink Grapefruit and Jicama Slaw next to each rice cake. Fill four small Asian sauce cups with the Asian Dipping Sauce and set on plates. Then brush each ahi skewer with a very light amount of vegetable oil and place skewers on a hot grill. Grill for about 1 minute per side. The ahi should be served rare. Place one skewer of ahi on each bed of slaw. Sprinkle with a pinch of thinly sliced green onion and serve.

SEARED FLATIRON STEAK SATAY

This is another version of a satay. The elements are flatiron steak, Crispy Chinese Egg Noodle Cake, Pickled Cucumber and Sweet Onion Relish, and Peanut Dipping Sauce.

Makes 4 servings

For the Peanut Dipping Sauce:

1   cup Vintage Basic Asian Marinade (see page 29)

1   tablespoon creamy peanut butter

1   tablespoon Asian black vinegar or balsamic vinegar

1   tablespoon Asian Kung Pao sauce (you can find this in the Asian section of most supermarkets)

1   tablespoon thinly sliced green onions

    Pinch of red chile flakes

For the Pickled Cucumber and Sweet Onion Relish:

1   small cucumber peeled, cored, and thinly sliced

½   small sweet onion (such as Walla Walla or Vidalia), very thinly sliced

1   tablespoon snipped fresh basil

2   tablespoons seasoned rice vinegar

2   teaspoons sugar

For the Crispy Chinese Egg Noodle Cakes:

2   cups cooked Chinese egg noodles

2   tablespoons thinly sliced green onions

2   teaspoons toasted sesame seeds

1   tablespoon salad oil

For the Satay:

1   1-pound piece flatiron steak

¼   cup Vintage Basic Asian Marinade (see page 29)

8   6-inch wooden skewers, soaked in water

To make the dipping sauce, blend Vintage Basic Asian Marinade, peanut butter, vinegar, and Asian Kung Pao sauce in a blender. Remove to a small bowl and add green onions and chile flakes; set aside.

To make the relish, mix all ingredients together in a bowl and refrigerate until ready to serve.

To make the egg noodle cakes, toss the noodles, green onions, and sesame seeds together in a bowl with the oil. Heat a 12-inch sauté pan over medium heat with a light coating of oil. Divide the noodle mixture into four portions and drop them into the hot sauté pan; cook for about 2 minutes per side. They will turn a nice golden brown and will be crispy. Make cakes right before you cook the flatiron satay.

To make the satay, marinate flatiron steak in Vintage Basic Asian Marinade for 30 minutes. Drain marinade and thinly slice the flatiron across the grain of the meat into 8 slices. Thread steak pieces onto skewers, one piece per skewer.

To finish the dish, set up four plates with a small sauce-cup of Peanut Dipping Sauce and a small sauce-cup of Pickled Cucumber and Sweet Onion Relish on each plate. When the noodle cakes are almost done put the flatiron satays on a hot grill and cook for about 1 minute per side. Just turn them once. (If you like your meat cooked more, leave them on a little longer.) Put one finished noodle cake on each plate beside the cups of condiments and place two skewers on each cake. Then serve. These are delicious. Enjoy!

Asian Sashimi Bruschetta

These are great little bites to get your meal going. They are kind of cross-cultural, but they work together really well. The warm bread soaked with Asian Vinaigrette is delicious all by itself. Topped with slaw and thin slices of raw sashimi-grade tuna, it is amazing. Here's what to do.

Makes 6 servings (2 each)

Asian Vinaigrette (see page 60)

12 slices fresh baguette, ⅓ inch thick each

12 tablespoons Asian Slaw (see page 76)

24 thin slices of raw sashimi-grade tuna (2 per bruschetta)

Wasabi Vinaigrette (see page 62)

Toasted sesame seeds

To assemble bruschettas, squirt a little Asian Vinaigrette on each bread slice. Grill bread face-down on the grill for 1 minute; turn over and grill for an additional 30 seconds. Place 2 slices of bread on each serving plate, put a tablespoon dollop of Asian Slaw on each piece of bread, and top with 2 thin slices of sashimi. Drizzle on a few drops of Wasabi Vinaigrette and sprinkle each with a pinch of toasted sesame seeds.

salads and dressings

■ ■ ■ ■

Salads and dressings express energy in an immediate and accessible form. The tastes are right up front. The textures are crisp and fresh and crunchy. Salads energize a meal immediately. They add a little POP to your being. There's no waiting around with a good salad. It's going to happen right now! My salads are all about electric energy. They are a little shock, a little thunder and lightning before the rain.

First, I'm going to give you our salad dressing and vinaigrette recipes. Use them with any green salad mix or vegetable combination that seems appealing to you. The dressings and vinaigrettes are also good with grilled or roasted vegetables. If you combine one of the dressings with a green salad mix, roasted potatoes, and slices of BBQ or grilled meat, you will have a refreshing and uplifting meal. I love the combination of hot and cold elements bound together by a vigorous dressing or lively vinaigrette. Here's to good eating!

A note on salad green proportions: I like to measure the salad greens by the handful. One medium handful of greens equals one serving. I also like to use 1 to 1½ tablespoons of dressing for each handful of greens. These are the proportions we'll use in the recipes.

ORANGE PECAN DRESSING

This dressing has been my favorite for the last year. Forget the salad for now. Just put some on the closest thing to you and eat it!

Makes 1½ cups

- 3 tablespoons seasoned rice vinegar
- ⅓ cup orange blossom honey
- 1 teaspoon fresh grated orange zest
- 3 tablespoons fresh orange juice
- ½ cup light olive oil or vegetable oil
- ¼ cup toasted and chopped pecans

Add the first five ingredients in order to a mixing bowl and whisk with a wire whip until honey has dissolved and blended with other ingredients. Add pecans. This dressing will keep for 2 to 3 weeks in the refrigerator.

SESAME MINT DRESSING

This dressing will take you from the exotic street markets of Marseille to the mistral winds of North Africa. I like to take trips with food. This dressing will take you on one.

Makes 1¼ cups

- 3 tablespoons red wine vinegar
- 3 tablespoons seasoned rice vinegar
- 2 teaspoons brown sugar
- ½ teaspoon salt
- ½ teaspoon whole fennel seed
- 1 teaspoon fresh grated ginger
- 1 tablespoon fresh crushed mint leaves
- 1 tablespoon plus 1 teaspoon lightly toasted sesame seeds
- ½ cup light olive oil

Add ingredients in order given to a mixing bowl. Blend well and chill. This dressing holds up nicely in a glass jar in the refrigerator.

Fresh Basil and Parmesan Vinaigrette

This dressing is great for summer pasta salads. Just get out the penne, olives, and tomatoes and you are home free.

Makes 2½ cups

½ cup red wine vinegar

1 tablespoon plus 1 teaspoon Dijon mustard

4 medium cloves garlic, smashed and then minced

½ tablespoon dry whole-leaf oregano

1 teaspoon kosher salt

1 teaspoon dry mustard powder

½ teaspoon fresh ground black pepper

¼ cup fresh finely snipped basil leaves

1 teaspoon fine lemon zest

4 tablespoons fresh shredded Parmesan cheese

1 good squeeze of ½ lemon

1½ cups light olive oil or vegetable oil

Mix all ingredients in a mixing bowl except the oil. Then drizzle in the oil. Shake vinaigrette well before you add to salad. Use 1 to 2 tablespoons dressing for each salad, or to taste. It will keep in the refrigerator for 2 to 3 weeks.

Creamy Mustard Dressing

This dressing is direct from The Copper Kettle, 1969, Aspen, Colorado. I include it here because I still love it and use it at Vintage. I also include it to remember Sarah Armstrong, in thanks for all she taught me.

Makes 1½ cups

2 hard-boiled eggs

1 to 1½ teaspoons kosher salt (to taste)

1½ teaspoons sugar

1 teaspoon ground black pepper

1 tablespoon chopped parsley

1 tablespoon Dijon mustard

1 large clove garlic, smashed

½ cup light olive oil

¼ cup red wine or seasoned rice vinegar

5 tablespoons cream or milk

Add ingredients in order given to a blender and blend until smooth. Dressing will keep for 2 to 3 weeks in the refrigerator.

CHIPOTLE-LIME RANCH DRESSING

This dressing is fast and easy and adds a nice south-western tang to a salad. It goes great with smoky BBQ chicken breasts sliced over a fresh green salad.

Makes about 1 cup

1	cup ranch dressing
1½	teaspoons chipotle Mexican hot sauce (you can find this in the Mexican section of most supermarkets)
4	teaspoons fresh lime juice

Blend all ingredients. Dressing will keep in the refrigerator for 2 to 3 weeks.

NEW ORLEANS SLAW DRESSING

This dressing is refreshing in a big and bold way. I use it when I'm serving smoky mixed grills, southern ribs, or blackened meats or fish.

Makes about 2 cups

1½	cups mayonnaise
½	cup real apple cider vinegar
⅓	cup sugar
1 to 2	teaspoons Vintage Spice Mix (see page 27)

Whisk all ingredients together in a bowl. Chill. Will store in refrigerator for 2 to 3 weeks.

BLUE CHEESE VINAIGRETTE

It seems like most blue cheese dressings are creamy dressings. My approach is a little different. This simple vinaigrette sets off the blue cheese. That's the way I like it.

Makes 3 cups

½ cup red wine vinegar

2 cloves garlic, minced

2 teaspoons dried basil leaves

1 to 1½ teaspoons kosher or sea salt

1 teaspoon dry mustard powder

½ teaspoon fresh ground black pepper

1 good squeeze of ½ lemon

1½ cups light olive oil or vegetable oil

1 cup of your favorite crumbled blue cheese

Add ingredients in order given, whisking in oil and then adding blue cheese last. Store in the refrigerator for 2 to 3 weeks.

For a nice variation, substitute dry oregano leaves or dry thyme leaves for the basil. In this type of vinaigrette, I also love to snip in fresh herbs. Try basil, oregano, thyme, or the one we all take for granted—parsley. It's really good.

VINTAGE BASIC VINAIGRETTE

This is simple and easy to make. It's great with greens, and I use it often to marinate boiled artichokes, braised fennel root, grilled veggies off the BBQ, and fresh-seared bread croutons in Italian-inspired bread salads. Just drizzle some on a good tomato. You won't regret it.

Makes 2 cups

½ cup red wine vinegar

1 tablespoon freshly squeezed lemon juice

2 cloves garlic, smashed and then minced

2 teaspoons dry leaf oregano

1 to 1½ teaspoons kosher salt (to taste)

1 teaspoon dry mustard powder

½ teaspoon fresh ground black pepper

1½ cups light olive oil or vegetable oil

Mix all ingredients together in a bowl except the oil. Whisk in the oil. Chill. Vinaigrette will keep in the refrigerator for 2 to 3 weeks.

Chile-Lime Vinaigrette

I use this vinaigrette to add a Latin touch to any salad or grilled vegetable combination.

Makes 1½ cups

- 4 tablespoons fresh lime juice
- 1 tablespoon red wine vinegar
- 2 cloves garlic, smashed and then minced
- 2 tablespoons diced sweet Walla Walla onion
- 2 tablespoons minced fresh cilantro
- 2 tablespoons minced fresh basil
- ½ teaspoon cayenne pepper
- 1 teaspoon toasted ground cumin seeds
- 1½ fresh jalapeño peppers, diced
- ½ teaspoon kosher salt
- ¼ teaspoon fresh ground black pepper
- 1 cup light olive oil or vegetable oil

Put all ingredients in an electric blender except the oil. Put on the lid and blend on medium speed. Drizzle in the oil through the hole in the lid. Blend for a few seconds more. Store in refrigerator for 2 to 3 weeks.

Asian Vinaigrette

This vinaigrette is fantastic to drizzle over green salad mixes to add an Asian accent.

Makes 1¾ cups

- 1 cup light olive oil
- 1 tablespoon sesame oil
- 10 cloves garlic
- 1¼ tablespoons dark brown sugar
- ¾ cup seasoned rice vinegar

Put olive oil and sesame oil in a small sauté pan with garlic cloves. Heat oil until garlic begins to simmer. Let the mixture simmer slowly for about 7 to 8 minutes, until the garlic just begins to turn golden. Remove from heat. In a small bowl, dissolve brown sugar in vinegar. After the oil mixture cools down, strain out the garlic cloves and add the oil to the vinegar. You now have a very nice basic Asian vinaigrette. This will keep in the refrigerator for 2 to 3 weeks.

ASIAN SESAME VINAIGRETTE

This one is too easy. Make the dressing and add it to a salad. I'll meet you in Bangkok!

Makes 2 cups

2   tablespoons lightly toasted sesame seeds

2   tablespoons very thin diagonally sliced green onions

    Pinch red chile flakes

1   tablespoon thinly sliced fresh basil leaves

1   recipe Asian Vinaigrette (see page 60)

Whisk sesame seeds, green onions, chile flakes, and basil into Asian Vinaigrette. Store in the refrigerator for 2 to 3 weeks.

BALSAMIC VINAIGRETTE

This is the Italian version of the Asian Vinaigrette. Use it as a dressing for green salad, grilled or roasted vegetables, or a plate of sliced heirloom tomatoes.

Makes 1¾ cups

1   cup light olive oil

10   cloves garlic

1¼ tablespoons dark brown sugar

¾   cup balsamic vinegar

Put olive oil in a small sauté pan with garlic cloves. Heat oil until garlic begins to simmer. Let the mixture simmer slowly for about 7 to 8 minutes, until the garlic just begins to turn golden. Remove from heat. In a small bowl, dissolve brown sugar in vinegar. After the oil mixture cools down, strain out the garlic cloves and add the oil to the vinegar. This is an excellent balsamic vinaigrette. It will keep for 2 to 3 weeks in the refrigerator.

WASABI VINAIGRETTE

This is a beautiful, spicy, light green dressing for salads, sashimi, or delicious roasted potatoes. Use your imagination for other dishes.

Makes 2 cups

2   tablespoons wasabi powder
2   tablespoons water
1   recipe Asian Vinaigrette (see page 60)

Mix the wasabi powder with the water to make a paste. Put Asian Vinaigrette and wasabi paste into a blender. Put on the lid and blend on medium speed for a few seconds. Vinaigrette will store for 2 to 3 weeks in the refrigerator.

WARM SHIITAKE MUSHROOM SESAME VINAIGRETTE

Serve this vinaigrette with Asian greens and bean sprouts or a spinach and watercress salad with orange wedges and sliced sweet onion. Toss in some grilled shrimp or thinly sliced grilled chicken breast and sprinkle on some honey roasted peanuts. You'll be over the moon.

Makes 1 cup

1   cup thinly sliced shiitake mushrooms
2   teaspoons olive oil
6   tablespoons Asian Sesame Vinaigrette (see page 61)

Sauté mushrooms in the slightest amount of oil for about 2 minutes. Pour Asian Sesame Vinaigrette over mushrooms and immediately toss with salad greens.

Vintage House Salad

I like a really good simple salad. It doesn't need to be overproduced. Just fresh crispy greens and a few colorful garnishes with a great vinaigrette or dressing is very satisfying. At Vintage, we always use a mixture of young organic salad greens called spring mix. It includes baby red and green romaine, oakleaf, baby spinach, baby red and green chard, arugula, and butterleaf. You can make your own mixture depending on what you find available, or just use one great lettuce.

Makes 4 servings

4	handfuls of salad greens
1	medium-size red bell pepper, cut in long thin strips
½	sweet onion, thinly sliced
8	small mushrooms (I prefer shiitake), thinly sliced
8	diagonal slices sweet cucumber
2	medium-size vine-ripe tomatoes, sliced into 8 wedges each
1 to 2	tablespoons freshly snipped herbs, such as basil, tarragon, chervil, parsley, or a combination of these
	About 6 tablespoons of any Vintage salad dressing (see pages 56 thru 61)

To make the salad, place the dressing in the bottom of a large bowl. You can use more or less to taste. Add the greens and vegetables to the bowl and toss the salad from the bottom up, gently, until the salad is just coated with the dressing. Don't overtoss the salad; use a light touch. You don't want to beat it up.

Serve the salad mounded up lightly on four cold salad plates. Serve with some warm bread and a glass of wine and enjoy.

Butterleaf, Fresh Pear, and Gorgonzola Salad

This may be the most refreshing salad I've ever made. We offer it as an off-menu special and we serve a ton. It's simplicity at its best.

Makes 4 servings

- 1 good squeeze of ½ lemon
- 1 fresh pear, peeled, cored, and thinly sliced
- 4 handfuls torn butterleaf lettuce
- 4 ounces crumbled Gorgonzola cheese
- 6 tablespoons Orange Pecan Dressing (see page 56)

Squeeze lemon juice over pear slices. Make sure lettuce is clean and dry. You don't want any grit in your salad. Put lettuce in a bowl with Gorgonzola and toss lightly with dressing. Pile the salad onto four chilled salad plates. Fan one-fourth of the sliced pear over each salad and drizzle a little more dressing over the top.

HEIRLOOM TOMATO SALAD

Any type of real vine-ripe tomato is good in this salad. Heirloom Tomato Salad is also great incorporated in other dishes, such as a topping for grilled meats or pizza. Serve a little of it warmed, with a squeeze of fresh orange juice and a pat of unsalted butter, to accompany grilled or oven-roasted fish fillets. Serve with sweet corn risotto or luscious Parmesan smashed potatoes.

Makes 4 servings

4   medium-size heirloom tomatoes, cut in ½-inch coarse dice

½   sweet onion, diced

3   tablespoons snipped fresh sweet basil

1½ tablespoons drained capers

Salt and fresh ground black pepper to taste

2   tablespoons extra-virgin olive oil

1   good squeeze of ½ lemon

2   small handfuls mixed lettuce greens

1   ripe avocado, pitted, peeled, and cut into quarters

2   tablespoons Vintage Basic Vinaigrette (see page 59)

In a bowl, combine tomatoes, onion, basil, capers, salt, pepper, oil, and lemon. Sprinkle lettuce greens equally around four chilled salad plates. Place one avocado quarter in the center of the greens on each plate. Now spoon the tomato mixture equally onto the avocado quarters. To finish, drizzle ½ tablespoon Vintage Basic Vinaigrette onto lettuce greens on each plate. Serve immediately.

Heirloom Tomato Bread Salad

Serve this recipe as a salad or use as an accompaniment to meat, such as grilled steak or lamb, with lemony white beans.

Makes 4 servings

16 1-inch coarse-cut chunks sourdough French bread

  Olive oil

  Drizzle of Vintage Basic Vinaigrette (see page 59)

1 recipe Heirloom Tomato Salad (see page 65)

16 kalamata olives, pitted

Drizzle bread with a little olive oil and then toast in the oven at 375 degrees F until crispy, yet still a little soft in the middle. Drizzle toasted bread with a little Vintage Basic Vinaigrette. Toss with Heirloom Tomato Salad and olives. Serve.

Mediterranean Salad

This salad is a simple combination of fresh tastes from the Mediterranean coastline. It is very versatile; it's good as a straight salad or as an accompaniment to grilled fish.

Makes 4 servings

1	artichoke
	Drizzle of Vintage Basic Vinaigrette (see page 59)
½	sweet onion, thinly sliced
1	red bell pepper, seeded and sliced length-wise
2	small fennel bulbs, shaved very thin
1	navel or blood orange (or 1 Mineola tangerine), peeled, seeded, and sliced in wedges
16	kalamata olives, pitted
1	thinly sliced green onion
2	tablespoons snipped fresh sweet basil, plus more for serving
	Pinch kosher salt
	Pinch fresh ground black pepper
1½	tablespoons olive oil
1	good squeeze of ½ lemon
2	small handfuls mixed salad greens

Quarter artichoke and steam until tender. When cool enough to handle, remove the choke. Drizzle with a little Vintage Basic Vinaigrette and refrigerate.

Put onion, bell pepper, fennel, orange, olives, green onion, basil, salt, and pepper in a bowl and toss with oil and a good squeeze of lemon to taste.

To serve, divide salad greens onto four chilled salad plates. Drizzle with a little Vintage Basic Vinaigrette. Place an artichoke quarter over the greens on each plate; spoon the Mediterranean mixture over artichoke and greens. Sprinkle more freshly snipped basil over each salad and serve.

Spicy King Crab Salad with Romaine, Tomato, and Cucumber

King crabmeat is often overlooked for use in salads and crab cakes. But I love it because it is so rich and sweet. This salad makes great use of king crabmeat. Paired with the other elements here, it makes a great dish.

Makes 4 servings

For Salad:

1   head romaine lettuce

1   cup firmly packed king crabmeat

2   ripe tomatoes, sliced about ¼ inch thick (Use 2 different colored tomatoes for a nice look)

8   diagonal slices cucumber

    Drizzle of Creamy Mustard Dressing (see page 57)

For Spicy Mayonnaise:

½   cup mayonnaise

½   teaspoon Vintage Spice Mix (see page 27)

1   tablespoon finely minced celery

1   tablespoon finely minced red bell pepper

1   tablespoon finely minced sweet onion

To make salad, peel off outer leaves of romaine and cut the stem out. Discard. Wash romaine under cold running water to remove any dirt or grit. Let the lettuce dry thoroughly. When it's dry, cut romaine into quarters lengthwise. If the lettuce is still wet, pat dry with paper towels.

Make the Spicy Mayonnaise by stirring together all ingredients until well blended.

In a bowl, mix king crabmeat with 4 teaspoons Spicy Mayonnaise. Now you can assemble the salad.

Place a wedge of romaine on the left side of each of four chilled salad plates. To the right of each plate, layer 2 tomato slices and 2 cucumber slices. Mound one-fourth of the king crab mixture in the center of each plate. Drizzle each salad with 1 to 2 tablespoons Creamy Mustard Dressing and serve.

Note: If the heads of romaine are quite large, divide them into 5 to 8 wedges instead of 4. Use your own judgment about the portion size.

GRILLED CHILE-LIME PRAWN SALAD

This salad is so versatile. You can have it as a salad course or you can add oven-roasted potato wedges and have a great dinner entrée.

Makes 2 servings

1	bunch fresh watercress or baby spinach, or a combination of both
8	16/20 size shrimp
	Light olive oil
	Vintage Spice Mix (see page 27)
1	red bell pepper, stemmed, seeded, and cut into ½-inch slices
1	yellow bell pepper, stemmed, seeded, and cut into ½-inch slices
½	small sweet red onion, cut into wedges
	Pinch kosher salt
2	green onions, cut in 2-inch sections
⅓	cup kalamata olives, pitted
	Chile-Lime Vinaigrette (see page 60)
1	tablespoon snipped fresh oregano
1	tablespoon snipped fresh cilantro

Wash greens and pat dry with a paper towel. Keep cold in the refrigerator in a mixing bowl.

Peel and devein shrimp, but leave on tails. Toss shrimp with the slightest amount of oil and a sprinkling of Vintage Spice Mix. Toss bell peppers and red onion in the slightest amount of oil and a pinch of kosher salt. Brush green onions with a tiny amount of oil. The shrimp and vegetables are now ready to grill.

Set grill or BBQ on medium-high. Grill shrimp and veggies, except green onions, for about 5 minutes, turning them over twice. Add green onions for the last 2 minutes only. When shrimp and vegetables are ready, put them in the bowl with the greens. Add olives and toss everything gently with 2 to 3 tablespoons of Chile-Lime Vinaigrette. (You can use more or less vinaigrette to taste.)

Divide the salad in equal portions on two salad plates. Sprinkle with the snipped oregano and cilantro.

JEFF'S QUINTESSENTIAL ITALIAN PASTA SALAD

Why do I call this salad quintessential Italian? Because it is simple and straightforward, not fussy. And because it has penne, salami, basil, olives, tomatoes, and a great vinaigrette. If this salad doesn't make you feel Italian, nothing will.

Makes 4 servings

2	cups uncooked penne pasta
	Olive oil
24	thin slices real Italian salami
1	cup feta cheese
⅔	cup pitted Italian black and green olives, mixed
1	cup tiny organic sweet cherry tomatoes
½	cup sliced sweet red onion
½	cup freshly snipped sweet basil
1	tablespoon drained capers
	Fresh wild mushrooms, (optional)
4	tablespoons Fresh Basil and Parmesan Vinaigrette (see page 57)
½	cup fresh grated Parmesan cheese

Cook penne pasta in a large pot of lightly salted boiling water until it is al dente. Drain it through a colander and rinse with cold water. Toss with a little olive oil so the pasta doesn't stick together; let it cool in a large bowl. Right before serving, add salami, feta cheese, olives, tomatoes, onion, basil, capers, and mushrooms, if using. Add vinaigrette and toss gently. Divide the salad between four chilled salad plates or bowls and sprinkle with fresh Parmesan.

Warm Fingerling Potato Salad

I like this salad because it combines the elements of hot and cold where the flavors meet in an unusual and nice place. I like to serve it as a salad. It's also great as a condiment for Asian steak salad with Warm Shiitake Mushroom Sesame Vinaigrette (see page 62) or with Asian marinated grilled fish.

Makes 4 servings

Olive oil

16 fingerling potatoes

Pinch kosher salt

1 bunch watercress

1 handful baby spinach

2 blood oranges, peeled, seeded, and cut into 16 wedges

½ medium-size sweet white onion, thinly sliced

Warm Shiitake Mushroom Sesame Vinaigrette (see page 62) or Sesame Mint Dressing (see page 56)

Lightly oil the potatoes and sprinkle with a little kosher salt. Roast in the oven at 375 degrees F for about 40 minutes or until fork-tender. Toss the remaining ingredients in a mixing bowl.

For an Asian-style salad, use Warm Shiitake Mushroom Sesame Vinaigrette. For a North African taste, drizzle with Sesame Mint Dressing.

Just to blow the lid off, add 16 ¼-inch chunks of Montrachet goat cheese and use Orange Pecan Dressing (see page 56).

JEFF'S FRENCH GIRLFRIEND'S HAM, ARTICHOKE, AND MUSHROOM SALAD

Yes, she really existed. It was 1978, Crested Butte, Colorado. And she could cook. You'd go over to Jeff's house—that's Jeff Hermanson, my partner in a little restaurant in Crested Butte—and immediately upon walking in his front door you'd be hit in the face by luxurious aromas wafting down from his kitchen, and you'd know that Collette was up there slow-cooking something that would take all day. She would cook a dish so slow that you couldn't see that it was cooking, and then at dinner you'd wish you could eat all night. It was sad when they split up, but I still remember the food. Make this salad and then mix it with equal parts penne pasta for a delicious pasta salad, or with equal parts boiled potatoes for a great potato salad.

Makes 4 to 5 servings

2 cups quartered canned artichoke hearts

2 cups quartered domestic button mushrooms

1½ tablespoons Dijon mustard

6 tablespoons Vintage Basic Vinaigrette (see page 59)

2 cups good-quality ham, cut in ½-inch cubes

1 tablespoon minced parsley

2 tablespoons snipped fresh basil

Drain artichoke hearts of their juices. Clean any dirt off the mushrooms with a brush or paper towel. Mix mustard with vinaigrette. Then simply put all of the ingredients in a bowl and toss gently.

If you want to make the penne or potato salad with this mixture, the proper proportions are 1 cup salad to 1 cup penne or potatoes and 1 ounce of dressing. Feel free to use more or less dressing according to your taste.

Asian Slaw

This is a simple and tasty little slaw that I use to accompany smoky pork tenderloin or ribs that have been marinated with Asian marinade, cold smoked, and then grilled. It's also good on thin grilled bread with sashimi-grade raw tuna or as an accompaniment to various satays.

Makes 4 to 6 servings

4 cups thinly sliced Nappa cabbage

½ cup very thin carrot matchsticks

¾ cup peeled, halved, and thinly sliced cucumber

½ cup very thinly sliced sweet onion

2 tablespoons very thinly sliced sweet basil

1 tablespoon sugar

3 tablespoons seasoned rice wine vinegar

Refrigerate all ingredients until cold. Put the first five ingredients into a bowl, sprinkle on sugar, and then lightly toss with rice wine vinegar.

Tropical Mango, Jicama, and Pineapple Slaw

This slaw is very refreshing and goes great with any game fish from tropical waters or halibut from Alaska.

Makes 4 to 6 servings

1 ripe mango, peeled, seeded, and sliced lengthwise

1 cup ½-inch slices pineapple

¾ small jicama, peeled and cut into matchsticks

½ cup thinly sliced Nappa cabbage

⅓ cup diagonally sliced green onions

½ jalapeño pepper, diced fine

1 teaspoon sugar

Juice of 1 medium-size lime

To make the slaw, prepare the first six ingredients. Refrigerate until cold. Put ingredients into a bowl, sprinkle on sugar, and squeeze on lime juice. Toss very gently.

Spicy New Orleans Slaw

Serve this slaw as an accompaniment to smoky BBQ meats, caramelized yams, pork chops smothered in Cajun gravy, spicy fried chicken, buttery smashed potatoes, or any down-home country food.

Makes 4 servings

- **3** cups thinly sliced Nappa cabbage
- ¾ cup diced sweet onion
- ¾ cup thinly sliced pineapple
- ½ cup very thin carrot matchsticks
- ⅓ to ½ cup New Orleans Slaw Dressing (see page 58)

Put all ingredients into a bowl and toss gently.

the lost art of great soup

■■■■

You have to care when you make soup. It's about chemistry and touch, and when I make soup I can feel it. I can see it in my mind before I make it. The chemistry is the ingredients—not so much the exact amounts, but how you put them together. That is the touch. It is all about capturing the flavor. That is the feel that comes to you in a vision, travels down through your arms and into your hands. It is how you handle the whole creative process. Making great soup is an art and a personal expression.

I first understood this years ago. It was a winter day, and I was out skiing with friends. I was young and didn't know much. But I loved the feeling of skiing—the movement, the speed, being on a mountain, pushing the envelope. Having the perception of the art of skiing—the relationship of the mountain and the snow and the skier—was a natural feeling. The spiritual connection was heavy with me, and I thrived being in that element. It all became one thing, oneness and peace.

Part of that equation in the best of times is having a great café on the mountain. You come in cold, hungry, at peace from the exercise, and the café wraps its welcoming arms around you. It's filled with thick, pungent air that smells of good food cooking. It was in this way that one day on a mountain in Colorado I came into a little café, simple but wonderful, and was slapped in the face by a magical cauldron of soup. It was sitting atop an open counter that you just went up to and helped yourself. I came up to it casually and looked in and was struck by the whole essence of what was in the pot. It was a cream soup like none I had ever seen before. It had an absolutely silken quality, a luster and aroma from another world. It was for me a mystical experience I'd never planned on having! After all, it was soup, and in my culture that had very little bearing. But it had a major effect on me that day. I, of course, had a bowl—probably two or three. It was rich with cauliflower and cabbage and carrots and parsley and potatoes and pepper. The silky cream broth was like a beautiful slippery lotion that caressed my mouth with layers of flavor and a smoothness I'd never experienced before. In that setting it was the most satisfying food I'd ever had up to that moment. For a short while I forgot about skiing, the mountains, my friends. I could only feel the effect the soup was having on my being. It stamped a message on my body and mind that will never go away.

Later, when I began my own restaurant, soup was something I always included on the menu. I always make one, two, or three soups a night. And the good thing about it is, it always brings back the feeling, that inner heat, of the first soup in the little mountain café. The other good thing is that through all these years our guests continue to love our soups. Over the years, as chefs try for ever more outrageous dishes and as trends come and go (most of which I ignore anyway), I make soup. It's the lost art of great soup. It's the art I discovered in myself that wintry day long ago in the high country of Colorado and that today forms the foundation of most of what I do in cooking.

■ ■ ■ ■

BAKED ONION AND ROASTED TOMATO SOUP

This soup combines the delicious elements of slowly sautéed yellow onions and oven-roasted, vine-ripe tomatoes to produce a simple, honest, heartwarming soup. Enjoy the layers of flavor that these simple techniques produce.

Makes 10 servings

6   Braised Garlic Cloves in Olive Oil
    (see page 28)

8   medium-size vine-ripe homegrown or
    heirloom tomatoes

4   medium yellow onions

2   tablespoons olive oil

¼   cup unsalted butter

2   tablespoons good quality unbleached
    white flour

1½ quarts chicken stock

1   cup dry white wine

¼   teaspoon dry whole-leaf thyme

¼   teaspoon fresh ground black pepper

    Pinch kosher salt

3   bay leaves

¾   cup freshly snipped basil, divided

10 thin slices sourdough baguette, lightly
    brushed with 1 tablespoon olive oil and
    toasted

    Grated Parmesan cheese

Heat an ovenproof cast-iron skillet with a light coating of garlic oil from the braised garlic. Sear tomatoes on all sides in skillet, and then drizzle with a tablespoon more olive oil from the braised garlic. Transfer skillet to an oven and bake for about 25 minutes at 400 degrees F. This will concentrate the flavor of the tomatoes and cook them enough so that the skins will peel right off. Remove tomatoes from oven and set aside. When they are cool enough to handle, simply pull off the skins and discard. Set tomatoes aside.

Peel onions and slice in half; then cut onions into thin slices. Heat a soup pot to medium-high and add 2 tablespoons of olive oil and the butter. Add sliced onions and cook them until they are soft, translucent, and buttery and are just turning a soft golden color. This brings out the natural sweetness and velvety flavor of the onions and releases that flavor into the oil and butter. (The trick now is to capture that flavor. It is the whole point of good cooking—knowing when that flavor has developed and then capturing it. As with most of the hot soups in this book, you capture the flavor at this point by adding the flour to the buttery onions.) Stir in flour and cook for about 2 minutes. All the delicious flavors you developed in the buttery onions will now be captured in the roux. Add chicken stock to onion mixture. The flavors of the onions will now be released into the stock; you will also have a slightly thickened texture that gives a nice body to the soup.

Add wine, thyme, pepper, salt, and bay leaves to the soup. Simmer uncovered for 30 minutes. To finish the soup, grind up tomatoes and braised garlic in a food processor. Add to the soup and

cook for about 5 more minutes. Stir in ½ cup of the freshly snipped basil.

To serve the soup, ladle 8-ounce ovensafe cups or bowls about three-fourths full. Place a toasted bread slice on top of each serving and sprinkle with about 2 tablespoons of grated Parmesan and a sprinkling of the remaining basil. Put each serving in the oven at 450 degrees F and bake for 2 minutes to melt cheese. Carefully remove the soup bowls from the oven and serve. This soup is great to serve over a few days, so store what you don't eat the first day in the refrigerator and simply heat it up and follow the serving process.

Spicy Tomato-Orange Soup with Peppery Orange Aioli

This is a wonderful variation of Baked Onion and Roasted Tomato Soup. Try this and you've made a little side trip to a village somewhere in Provence.

Makes 10 servings

6   Braised Garlic Cloves in Olive Oil (see page 28)

8   medium-size vine-ripe homegrown or heirloom tomatoes

4   medium yellow onions

2   tablespoons olive oil

¼   cup unsalted butter

2   tablespoons good quality unbleached white flour

1½   quarts chicken stock

1   cup red wine

¼   teaspoon dry whole-leaf thyme

¼   teaspoon fresh ground black pepper

     Pinch kosher salt

¼   teaspoon red chile flakes

1½   teaspoons whole fennel seeds

3   bay leaves

¾   cup freshly snipped basil, divided

     Finely grated zest of 1 orange

     Juice of 1 orange

10   thin slices sourdough baguette, lightly brushed with 1 tablespoon olive oil and toasted

     Peppery Orange Aioli (see page 27)

Heat an ovenproof cast-iron skillet with a light coating of garlic oil from the braised garlic. Sear tomatoes on all sides in skillet, and then drizzle with a tablespoon more olive oil from the braised garlic. Transfer skillet to an oven and bake for about 25 minutes at 400 degrees F. Remove tomatoes from oven and set aside. When they are cool enough to handle, simply pull off the skins and discard. Set tomatoes aside.

Peel onions and slice in half; then cut onions into thin slices. Heat a soup pot to medium-high and add 2 tablespoons of olive oil and the butter. Add sliced onions and cook them until they are soft, translucent, and buttery and are just turning a soft golden color. Stir in flour and cook for about 2 minutes. Add chicken stock to onion mixture. You will now have a slightly thickened texture that gives a nice body to the soup.

Add wine, thyme, pepper, salt, red chile flakes, fennel seeds, and bay leaves to the soup. Simmer uncovered for 30 minutes. To finish the soup, grind up tomatoes and braised garlic in a food processor. Add to the soup and cook for about 5 more minutes. Stir in ½ cup of the freshly snipped basil, orange zest, and orange juice. Finish the soup with the toasted crouton, a dollop of Peppery Orange Aioli, and a sprinkling of the remaining basil.

CREAM OF MUSHROOM AND FRESH HERB SOUP

I find that people never tire of mushroom soup. There must be an ancient gene in modern man that calls out when mushroom soup appears on the menu. It speaks to our lost connection to the soil, coming from the earth and returning to the earth. It speaks to the magical effect of the wild fungi on our brains and nervous systems and the dangerous side effects of getting the wrong mushroom. The mushroom embodies the big gamble and temptation of life, finding that safe place between ecstasy and death. In the modern and tamed world, when can we experience being wild and free again? Maybe that is the attraction of the mushroom. I know I am very attracted to these little magical creations. They are a mystical fascination and I never tire of cooking with them.

Makes 12 servings

½ cup unsalted butter

1 large yellow onion, diced

2 medium-size carrots, peeled, sliced thin on the diagonal, and then sliced into thin matchsticks

30 ounces button or crimini mushrooms, sliced (plus a few wild mushrooms, such as chanterelle or morel, thrown in for fun)

2 tablespoons good quality unbleached white flour

1½ quarts chicken stock

½ cup Madeira wine

½ teaspoon curry powder

½ teaspoon dry whole-leaf thyme

¼ teaspoon fresh ground black pepper

Pinch cayenne pepper

2 tablespoons chopped fresh parsley

3 cups heavy cream

2 tablespoons freshly snipped herbs such as dill, thyme, or basil

To make the soup, melt the butter in a medium-size soup pot and add in order the onion, carrots, and mushrooms. Sauté on low to medium heat for about 15 minutes, stirring frequently. Stir in the flour and cook the mixture for about 2 more minutes, stirring a few times. Add the chicken stock and Madeira. Add curry powder, thyme, pepper, cayenne pepper, and parsley. Stir until the mixture is well blended, and then bring the soup to a boil. Turn down the heat so the soup is at a high simmer and cook for about 30 minutes. You should now smell the exotic aroma of the mushrooms backed up by a strong foundation of the other ingredients. The soup should have a luscious viscosity but not be too thick.

Scald the cream in a separate pot by heating it until a wrinkled film forms over the top. Turn off the heat under the soup, and then add the cream to the soup and stir it in. Stir in freshly snipped herbs. You can add more or less herbs depending on your taste. Sprinkle a pinch of freshly snipped herbs over each serving.

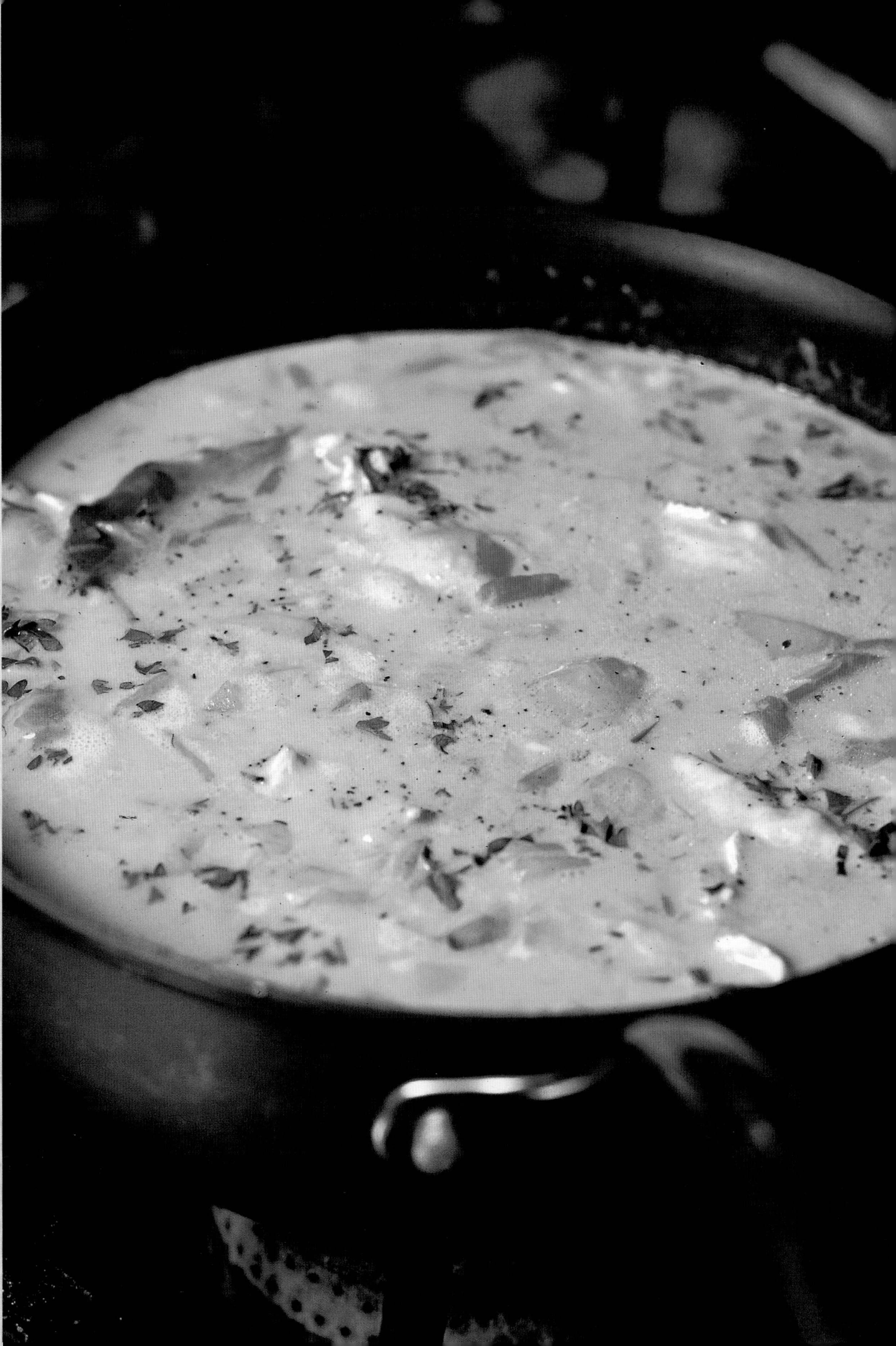

Leek, Brie, and Yukon Gold Potato Chowder

When I think of chowders, two places come to mind. New England for fish chowders that warm the soul when the cold wind blows in off the sea, and the Swiss and French Alps for big and rich cheesy chowders that warm the hearts of the mountain people. In both cases the basic elements are the same. They begin with butter, onions, potatoes, pepper, parsley, a good stock, and cream. Once you get that basic idea you'll have a sense of those cultures and you'll have a blast making the chowder.

Makes 12 servings

- 6   tablespoons unsalted butter
- 1   medium-size yellow onion, diced
- 2   small carrots, peeled, sliced thin on the diagonal, and then cut into thin matchsticks
- 4   leeks with the tough outer leaves removed, then sliced lengthwise, washed, and sliced thin
- 5   medium-size Yukon Gold potatoes, peeled, quartered, and cut into ¼-inch-thick slices
- 2   tablespoons good quality unbleached white flour
- 1½   quarts chicken stock
      Small pinch saffron threads
- ¼   teaspoon fresh ground black pepper
- ½   teaspoon dry whole-leaf thyme
- ⅓   cup chopped fresh parsley
- 2   bay leaves
- 2   cups heavy cream
- 6   ounces French Brie cheese, with the outer skin of the cheese on, cut in ½-inch cubes

Melt the butter in a medium-size soup pot. Add the onions, carrots, and leeks. Cook for about 5 minutes, stirring often, to soften the vegetables. Add the potatoes and cook for a few more minutes. Stir often. Add the flour, continuing to stir, and cook for a few more minutes. Add the chicken stock, saffron, pepper, thyme, parsley, and bay leaves. Stir until the chowder is well blended.

Bring the chowder to a boil, then turn it down to a nice medium simmer and cook for about 40 minutes. Stir it often to make sure nothing is sticking to the bottom of the pot. The chowder should have a beautiful viscosity and taste delicious. Scald the cream in a separate pot by heating it until a wrinkled film forms over the top. Turn off the heat under the chowder and add the scalded cream; stir it in thoroughly. Add the Brie and let it melt slowly. I like there to be nice soft pieces of the Brie floating in the chowder. It's wonderful that way. This hearty chowder makes a great meal when served with warm bread and a salad. Remove the bay leaves before serving.

Oyster Chowder

The Leek, Brie, and Yukon Gold Potato Chowder is such a quintessential chowder that by tweaking it a little bit you can make it into other great chowders. Oyster Chowder is one I like to make.

Makes 12 servings

24 fresh shucked oysters

1 recipe Leek, Brie, and Yukon Gold Potato Chowder (see page 87)

Add the oysters to the finished chowder and heat until the oysters are cooked through. Serve immediately, sprinkling the steaming Oyster Chowder with freshly chopped parsley.

Cajun Andouille Oyster Chowder

The sausage adds a knockout punch to this chowder.

Makes 12 servings

- 1   Cajun Andouille sausage
- 24   fresh shucked oysters
- 1   recipe Leek, Brie, and Yukon Gold Potato Chowder (see page 87)

Grill a Cajun Andouille sausage and then thinly slice it. Add it to the Leek, Brie, and Yukon Gold Potato Chowder when you add the oysters. It is so good!

Braised Garlic Chowder

The braised garlic in this recipe is mellow and buttery and adds a smooth garlic flavor to the chowder.

Makes 12 servings

- 20   Braised Garlic Cloves in Olive Oil (see page 28)
- 1   recipe Leek, Brie, and Yukon Gold Potato Chowder (see page 87)

Mash up braised garlic cloves and add them to the chowder when you add the stock. You might choose to leave out the Brie cheese in the end, but it's good either way. If you do leave out the Brie, add one extra cup of scalded cream to the chowder. Don't forget to sprinkle the chowder with fresh chopped parsley when you serve it.

ALPINE CHOWDER FROM ASPEN MEMORIES, THE MOTHER SOUP

This chowder is my homage to the pot of soup that slapped me across the kisser in that little mountainside café and woke me up to the possibilities of simple good eating. That soup had spirit and energy. I learned something that day. Here's one from the heart.

Makes 12 servings

½ cup unsalted butter

1½ medium yellow onions, diced

1 leek, white and tender inner green part only, washed and thinly sliced

2 medium carrots, peeled, sliced on the diagonal, and then cut into thin matchsticks

2 cloves garlic, smashed and diced

4 medium-size Yukon Gold potatoes, peeled, quartered, and sliced ¼ inch thick

2 tablespoons good quality unbleached white flour

1½ quarts chicken stock

1 head cauliflower, quartered, broken into florets, and thinly sliced

¼ teaspoon fresh ground black pepper

½ teaspoon dry whole-leaf thyme

Pinch saffron threads

2 bay leaves

⅓ cup chopped parsley

3 cups heavy cream

Finely grated zest of 1 medium-size orange

8 ounces grated medium-sharp cheddar cheese

Freshly snipped herbs, such as mixed parsley, dill, thyme, and basil

To make the chowder, melt butter in a medium-size soup pot, add onion, leek, carrots, and garlic and sauté for about 5 minutes, stirring frequently, until they become soft and their natural flavors are released. Stir in potatoes and cook for 2 more minutes. Stir in flour and cook for 2 more minutes. Add chicken stock and cauliflower.

Stir in all the herbs and spices until ingredients are well blended. Turn up the heat and let the chowder come to a boil. Turn down the heat immediately and cook the chowder on a medium simmer for about 40 minutes. Stir it every now and then to make sure nothing is sticking to the bottom of the pot. Scald the cream in a separate pot by heating it until a wrinkled film forms over the top. Turn off the heat under the chowder; add the scalded cream and stir until well blended.

On very low heat, add orange zest and grated cheddar cheese. Stir until the cheese has melted into the chowder and everything is well blended. Taste and adjust seasonings. I like a little more fresh ground black pepper in this one. Sprinkle each bowl of chowder with the snipped fresh herbs to serve.

SZECHWAN CARROT SOUP

This soup just tastes so healthy. It is alive with vital ingredients that will perk your energy level right up. If you are creating an Asian dinner, this soup would make a great starter.

Makes 8 servings

1   medium yellow onion, diced

1   fennel root bulb, washed and diced

2   cloves garlic, smashed and diced

20 ounces carrots, peeled and sliced

2   tablespoons peeled and thinly sliced fresh gingerroot

1½ tablespoons light vegetable oil

1   quart chicken or vegetable stock

⅛   teaspoon red chile flakes

1   teaspoon Sriracha (Asian chile sauce—you can find this at most supermarkets)

1   cup Thai coconut milk (you can find this in the Asian section of most supermarkets)

2   tablespoons Vintage Basic Asian Marinade (see page 29)

2   tablespoons creamy peanut butter

1   teaspoon toasted sesame oil

½   cup cream

To make the soup, sauté the first five ingredients with the vegetable oil in a small soup pot for about 5 minutes on medium-low heat. Stir frequently. Add stock, chile flakes, and Sriracha. Cook the soup on a low boil for about 35 minutes or until the vegetables are soft. Add coconut milk and cook for 5 more minutes. Add remaining ingredients and remove from heat. Let the soup cool a little. Puree the soup in small batches in your blender. At this point you can either reheat the soup and serve it, or let it cool completely and store to serve later. It stores well for a few days in the refrigerator. Just reheat and serve. I like to serve this soup garnished with pickled ginger and freshly snipped basil or with grilled thin slices of smoked Muscovy duck breast and Asian sliced green onions.

CREAMY BAKED ONION SOUP WITH GRILLED MUSHROOMS

This is a soup to warm you up during cold weather. I like the earthiness that the grilled mushrooms add to the creamy onions. The white wine, black pepper, and fresh tarragon cut through it all and the fresh mozzarella adds a double dose of decadence. A glass of champagne goes well with this soup.

Makes 12 servings

4 to 5 medium-size yellow or white onions, peeled, cut in half, and thinly sliced

5 green onions, washed, dried, and thinly sliced

7 tablespoons unsalted butter

2½ tablespoons good quality unbleached white flour

1 cup dry white wine

1½ quarts chicken or vegetable stock

4 bay leaves

¼ teaspoon dry whole-leaf thyme

¼ teaspoon fresh ground black pepper

2 cups heavy cream

1 pound sliced mushrooms (a combination of crimini, shiitake, and morel)

Pinch kosher salt

Pinch fresh ground black pepper

Drizzle of olive oil

1½ tablespoons freshly snipped French tarragon

12 thin baguette slices, brushed with olive oil and toasted on the grill or in the oven

12 ¼-inch slices of fresh mozzarella

Cook onions slowly in butter in a soup pot until they are meltingly soft. Don't rush. Add flour and cook for a few more minutes, stirring frequently. Add wine and stock and stir until combined. Add bay leaves, thyme, and pepper; simmer for 30 to 40 minutes. Scald the cream in a separate pot by heating it until a wrinkled film forms over the top. Turn off the heat under the soup; add the scalded cream and stir until well blended.

At this point put sliced mushrooms in a bowl and sprinkle them with a little kosher salt, pepper, and a drizzle of olive oil. Spread them out on a grill and cook them for about 1 minute on each side. When they are done, add them to the soup. (If you don't have a grill, put mushrooms in a large ovenproof sauté pan and roast them in an oven at 350 degrees F for 6 or 7 minutes.) Add tarragon to soup and stir. Heat the soup just to a simmer, and then turn off the heat. Remove bay leaves from the soup and discard.

To serve the soup, set your oven to 450 degrees F. Fill each cup or bowl three-fourths full. Put one crostini with one slice of mozzarella on top in the center of each soup. Put soup in the oven for about 2 to 3 minutes so the cheese begins to melt. Carefully remove each bowl and serve.

Avocado Gazpacho

I was raised in avocado country. There were avocado trees in our yard and in the surrounding hills. My parents loved them, and they had a constant presence on our kitchen table. I use avocados whenever I can at the restaurant. Sometimes I even make this gazpacho in the middle of winter if there is a threat of a warm spell.

Makes 10 to 12 servings

1½ quarts cold chicken or vegetable broth

3 large, perfectly ripe avocados

1 medium white or yellow onion, peeled and chopped

1 large sweet cucumber, peeled, seeded, and sliced

⅓ cup freshly snipped cilantro

⅓ cup freshly squeezed lime juice

1 teaspoon curry powder

1 to 2 teaspoons of your favorite hot sauce (I like Sriracha or sambal chile sauce)

¼ teaspoon fresh ground black pepper

¼ teaspoon kosher salt

Put the cold broth in a large stainless steel bowl. Cut the avocados in half, remove the pit, and scoop out the avocado into the broth. Add the remaining ingredients to the bowl. Now process the soup in small batches in your food processor. Don't make it too smooth. You want it a little crunchy. Adjust the seasonings to taste. I start out with a small amount of spice, so if it needs more, go for it. It may need a little more lime juice, a little more hot sauce, or a little more cilantro. Whatever you think. Chill the soup in the refrigerator until it is cold. I like to serve this gazpacho in chilled bowls or cups with a dollop of Vintage Pico de Gallo (see page 110) or Cabo Rock Shrimp Tomato Relish (see page 112).

SHELLFISH GAZPACHO

This soup is like a health-food drink served in a bowl! The ingredients are all vital and fresh and will do wonders for both body and mind. It's a great energizer on a hot summer's day.

Makes 10 servings

For the Gazpacho:

3   cups chicken, clam, or vegetable broth

3   cups tomato juice

1½   cucumbers, peeled, seeded, and diced

5   vine-ripe, medium-size tomatoes, coarsely chopped with their juice and seeds

1   medium-size sweet white or yellow onion, diced

1½   stalks celery, diced

3   tablespoons chopped parsley

2   medium-size cloves garlic, smashed and diced

1   red bell pepper, seeded and diced

1   green bell pepper, seeded and diced

¼   cup extra-virgin olive oil

¼   cup Italian red wine vinegar

1   cup prepared chile sauce

½   teaspoon kosher salt

½   teaspoon fresh ground black pepper

1   tablespoon freshly squeezed lemon juice

1   tablespoon Tabasco sauce

For the Shellfish:

20   fresh steamer clams, washed

     Drizzle white wine

     Drizzle lemon juice

20   fresh mussels, washed and debearded

16 to 20 medium-size shrimp

¾   cup freshly snipped basil

¾   cup thinly sliced green onions

To make the gazpacho, put all of the ingredients in a large bowl. You are now ready to process the soup. I like to do this in one of two ways depending on how I'm feeling. The first way is to process the mixture in small batches in a food processor, pulsing until it is chopped uniformly but still crunchy. The second way is to hand dice all of the vegetables and combine them with the rest of the ingredients. This makes a more rustic presentation which I like very much.

Once you have processed the gazpacho, put it in your refrigerator to chill. Chill for at least 2 or 3 hours. While it is chilling, prepare the shellfish. Put the steamer clams into a sauté pan, drizzle a little white wine and lemon juice over them, cover the pan and place it over high heat. Steam for about 2 minutes and the clams will open up. As they open, remove them from the pan and set on a plate. Discard any clams that won't open. Put all the opened clams in the refrigerator right away and chill them. Follow the exact same process with the mussels as for the clams. Peel the shrimp but leave the last section on the shell with the tail of the shrimp on. Steam or boil the shrimp just until they are done, about 2 to 3 minutes at the most. Put them on a plate in your refrigerator until thoroughly chilled.

When all the elements of the recipe are cold, you can serve the gazpacho. To serve, simply arrange 2 clams, 2 mussels, and 2 shrimp each in chilled soup bowls. Pour the gazpacho over the shellfish and give each bowl a little shake to settle the ingredients. Sprinkle each bowl with some basil and green onion and you are ready to serve. Enjoy some very healthy and happy eating!

tomato manifesto

■■■■

I decided to take a stand on tomatoes. I was tired of the disappointment every time I sliced a tomato for a salad, or made tomato chutney or pico de gallo. The tomatoes available from the produce company or the grocery store, stacked in anonymous boxes a mile high in warehouses, and then shipped hundreds (maybe thousands) of miles cross-country have no life and no inner energy. They have no discernable flavor, an artificial waxy skin, and a hard pulpy interior. They will never ripen and were grown for the qualities of long-distance shipping and long shelf life. They might as well be made of plastic. I guess we are so used to them that nobody ever questions it. But I did.

I remember walking around in my grandparents' garden as a kid. I was hunting. It was a search-and-destroy mission to find the monstrous tomato worm, that big, fat, greenish-blue monster with the sinister red hook-horn coming out of its head. It was so ugly and fascinating it intimidated the chickens—and me too! But it was my mission to get rid of them so that is what I did, with relish. The one thing I noticed and will always remember is the aroma of the tomato plants. It was rich and thick in the air and you could not keep from eating a few of the tomatoes while on the hunt. And the tomatoes had flavor—big delicious flavor. There was that magic chemistry between acidity and sweetness going on that made your mouth just burst alive. I'd salivate at the thought of it.

Today that experience has largely disappeared except for those lucky souls who grow their own gardens or seek out truck farms or roadside vegetable stands and eat real food with true flavor and texture that you don't find in the commercially grown produce that is commonly available. It saddens me to think that as a culture millions of people aren't even aware that their food could be so much better. We are a great nation at producing an abundance of food. We take pride in our bigness and power. Even tomatoes look nice on display at the grocery store. But it is superficial because below the surface all of the great qualities are missing: the aroma, the texture, the flavor, and probably even the nutrition. Does that say something in a larger sense about our nation? It's a question to ponder.

But the good news on the tomato front is this: you can have that full-flavor, mouth-bursting experience of a real ripe tomato. There is a movement coming alive in the United States. Many people are searching for better and more healthful food, and many growers are producing it. I often see a small section in the produce department devoted to organic or naturally raised vegetables. It often starts with a small box of heirloom tomatoes sitting over on the side somewhere, the produce person experimenting to see if anyone is interested. If enough people are interested maybe that little offering will get bigger and the section of industrially grown tomatoes will get smaller. But the movement happens in one-person increments. It begins with you and me simply turning away from mediocrity and superficiality. It begins by starting a dialogue with our produce person at the grocery store or produce company. I find that they love to hear what I have to say and are very cooperative about searching for the products I want. And naturally so, because that is their business. I think that they, too, are interested in better food and take pride in what they sell. It's a new adventure for them because they know that there are growers out there who are producing tomatoes bred for flavor and quality. They just need a little nudge in that direction and they will respond positively. Our responsibility is to support the grocer and the producer so that it is economically viable to grow and sell the produce. It is our responsibility to create a better culture for those who come after us, and food is certainly one place to start.

Now, when I make that salad, or tomato chutney, or pico de gallo, I'm proud to serve it. I'm proud to give better food to my customers and to my family. And I'm proud to support the agriculture that is producing that food.

This, of course, goes way beyond tomatoes. It includes all of our food and all of our agricultural system. It is going to be a slow evolution and a slow revolution. Institutions are hard to change, but there is nothing like the voice of the people to cause change in the corporate world. Speak with your actions and dollars. Board members understand that.

Stand up and walk away from the tasteless, the superficially pretty, the hollow hope of mere appearance and walk towards the delights and pleasures of the full flavored, the nutritious, the robust, the life affirming. You will know it when you experience it. It is a positive action, a quiet revolution, and a step towards making this a better world.

■ ■ ■ ■

Tricolored Vine-Ripe Tomato Salad

This salad is fundamental to the basic art of tomatoes. It's a simple chemistry that is the essence of the tomato itself. You can put it together five minutes before you need it, and it will be the freshest expression of the tomato that you have ever eaten.

Makes 4 to 6 servings

1	red vine-ripe tomato, heirloom if available
1	yellow vine-ripe tomato, heirloom if available
1	orange or green tomato, heirloom if available
½	sweet Italian red onion, yellow Walla Walla onion, or Vidalia onion
8	¼-inch slices fresh mozzarella (optional)
12	pitted kalamata olives (optional)
12	fresh orange wedges, peeled and seeded (optional)
1 to 2	tablespoons freshly snipped basil
1 to 2	teaspoons drained capers
2	teaspoons seasoned rice vinegar
1	tablespoon extra-virgin olive oil
	Pinch kosher salt
	Pinch fresh coarse ground black pepper

To make the salad, simply slice the tomatoes about ¼ inch thick and fan them out on a large dinner plate. Cut onion into very thin slices and lay lightly over tomatoes. Layer with optional ingredients, if using. Sprinkle with basil and capers. Drizzle on vinegar and olive oil. Sprinkle with salt and ground black pepper. Now gather round the plate and eat!

This salad also tastes great served on fresh-cut slices of baguette or spooned over lettuce greens that have been dressed with Balsamic Vinaigrette (see page 61). Use as a topping for a steak right off the grill. Or warm some up in a sauté pan with a little unsalted butter and a squeeze of orange juice and serve it over oven-roasted halibut or white sea bass. It's the theme of building with tomatoes.

JEFF'S MOST CLASSIC TOMATO SOUP

This soup is all about tomatoes and bringing the tomato flavor to its essence. It's not fancy or complicated, just simple and delicious.

Makes 6 to 8 servings

- 2 tablespoons garlicky olive oil from Braised Garlic Cloves in Olive Oil (see page 28)
- 2 pounds vine-ripe heirloom tomatoes
- 6 Braised Garlic Cloves (see page 28)
- Kosher salt and fresh coarse ground black pepper to taste
- 2 medium-size zucchini
- Olive oil
- 6 cups chicken broth or vegetable broth
- ½ cup freshly snipped basil leaves plus more for serving
- 6 to 8 slices of baguette cut ¼ inch thick

Preheat oven to 325 degrees F. Put the garlicky olive oil in a heavy ovenproof cast-iron skillet over high heat. Add the tomatoes and sear them for 2 to 3 minutes total, searing all sides. Remove skillet from heat and add braised garlic cloves. Sprinkle with salt and pepper. Place skillet in preheated oven and roast the tomatoes and garlic for 30 minutes. Remove skillet and let it cool just enough so you can handle the tomatoes. Pull skins off tomatoes; they should come off easily. The garlic cloves and tomatoes will be quite soft; mash them up with a fork.

Thinly slice zucchini lengthwise and brush strips with a light coating of olive oil and a little sprinkling of salt and pepper. Sear zucchini in a large sauté pan over medium-high heat. Cook for 1 minute per side, and then remove to a cutting board and cut on the diagonal into ½ inch widths. Add zucchini to skillet with tomato and garlic; cook the mixture for about 2 minutes while stirring.

Heat broth to a boil in a medium-size soup pot. Add the roasted tomato mixture, stirring until everything is thoroughly blended. Simmer the soup for 15 minutes over medium heat. Turn off the heat and stir in basil.

While the soup is cooking, brush each bread slice with a light coating of olive oil and sear in a hot sauté pan until lightly browned on the outside but still a bit soft on the inside. Set aside until the soup is finished. To serve, put a toasted bread slice in each soup bowl and then ladle in the hot soup. Sprinkle each serving with a little more snipped basil.

TOMATO AND BLACK CURRANT CHUTNEY

It's Crested Butte, Colorado, 1976, and I stumble into town with a college friend. I buy Soupcon, a little restaurant located in a converted log cowshed. The previous owner is Candy Durham, and she becomes my assistant chef. Candy taught me many things. One of them is the chemistry of chutney. Later on, in 1980, I sold Soupcon to Craig and Cindy Ling, a young couple from Baltimore. One of Craig's best dishes was his pecan-crust chicken with sour cream sauce. In 1985, Sheila and I started another Soupcon Restaurant in Ketchum, Idaho. That summer I borrowed the elements of Candy's tomato currant chutney and Craig's pecan-crust chicken, put them together, and Sun Valley Pecan-Crusted Chicken was born. I suppose this is the real story of how cooking is learned. It's a living process and takes in everything we experience in life. I do my own take on it at Vintage, which just happens to be located in the very cabin we restored twenty years ago for Soupcon. Here's that chutney recipe. The pecan chicken dish will follow in the Entrées chapter.

Makes about 3 cups

½   cup diced yellow onion

2   cloves garlic, smashed and then diced

7   bright red vine-ripe Roma tomatoes, coarsely chopped

½   teaspoon red chile flakes

¼   wedge of a lime, diced with peel on

¼   small orange, diced with peel on

1½ teaspoons chile powder

1   heaping tablespoon fresh grated ginger

¾   cup sugar

½   cup seasoned rice vinegar

¼   cup dry golden raisins

⅓   cup dry Zante currants

To make the chutney, put all the ingredients in a saucepan and, stirring everything together, bring to a high simmer and cook about 30 to 40 minutes until it reaches a nice jammy texture. Stir it up a few times while it cooks. Don't let it get too thick, as it will thicken a little more as it cools off. Let the chutney cool off and then store it in the refrigerator. It's best served cold. It goes great with Sun Valley Pecan-Crusted Chicken (see page 157), but is wonderful with any roasted meat, especially roast pork or fried pork chops. It really comes into its own when served as a condiment with lamb curry.

TOMATO GINGER JAM

This sweet treat with some background heat is a great little condiment to have around when you need to perk up a dish. A dollop adds a nice North African touch to rice or couscous served with a spicy roast chicken or with chops or a steak. Canned tomatoes can work very well when you can't find decent fresh tomatoes, so you can make Tomato Ginger Jam anytime. It stores great in the refrigerator and stays fresh for weeks when tightly covered.

Makes 1 pint

1   2½-pound can tomatoes and their juice or 2½ pounds fresh tomatoes

1¼ cups sugar

½   lemon, quartered and sliced thin with skin on

½   cup thinly sliced candied ginger

¼   teaspoon red chile flakes

Pinch cayenne pepper

Juice of ½ lemon

To make the jam, combine all of the ingredients in a stainless steel saucepan and cook over medium heat at a firm simmer until the mixture becomes nice and shiny and has a thick jammy texture. Stir it frequently so nothing sticks to the bottom of the pan. You don't want the sugar to burn. The jam is done when it has a luscious silken texture. This might take about 45 minutes. Keep an eye on it and don't forget to stir it up now and then. Store the jam in a clean glass jar with a lid.

Vintage Pico de Gallo

This is my favorite tomato condiment to have available on a daily basis. We use it with our tamales and our oysters at the restaurant, but I also take it home to use on scrambled eggs with spicy sausage, or to sprinkle over green salads. This is, of course, our own unique style of pico. It's kind of cross-cultural with Mexican and Provencal elements; it's fun to use to kick up all kinds of dishes.

Makes 3 cups

3	medium-size vine-ripe tomatoes, cut in ¼-inch square pieces
½	medium-size sweet onion, diced
1	jalapeño pepper, seeded and diced fine
2	tablespoons snipped cilantro leaves
1	tablespoon snipped mint leaves (or substitute 1 tablespoon snipped basil leaves)
1	tablespoon drained capers
1	tablespoon diced green onion
	Juice of 1 medium-size lime
	Pinch of salt, to taste
	Pinch of fresh ground black pepper

To make the pico, prepare the ingredients, then combine them in a mixing bowl and gently stir everything together. Don't over-handle because you don't want to break down the tomatoes. Use a light touch. The pico is now ready to eat. It is best the first day you make it, so use it up and make some more tomorrow.

HAIR-OF-THE-DOG DIPPING SAUCE

This one starts with our *Vintage Pico de Gallo*. It is hot and tasty and great for dipping chips or south-of-the-border chicken wings or for spooning on a street stand shrimp taco. Feel free to turn down the heat if it's too hot—that's okay by me. If you really like heat, add another 1/2 teaspoon habanero sauce.

Makes 2½ cups

2   cups Vintage Pico de Gallo (see page 110)
1   tablespoon tequila
½   teaspoon habanero chile sauce
1   tablespoon diced green onions
4   tablespoons sour cream

Gently combine all of the ingredients in a bowl and you are ready to burn!

Cabo Rock Shrimp Tomato Relish

We again use the Vintage Pico de Gallo to start this relish, but cut the tomatoes into 1/2-inch square pieces instead of 1/4-inch pieces. I like to use this relish as a garnish in my Avocado Gazpacho or spooned over grilled Sea of Cortez White Sea Bass. It's also great spooned on grilled bread as a little appetizer or palette cleanser.

Makes 4½ cups

1½ cups rock shrimp

2   teaspoons Vintage Spice Mix (see page 27)

2   tablespoons olive oil

1   recipe Vintage Pico de Gallo (see page 110)

1   tablespoon diced green onions

1   tablespoon freshly squeezed lime juice

To make the relish, sprinkle the rock shrimp with the Vintage Spice Mix and sauté the shrimp in the smallest amount of oil in a hot sauté pan until just done. Remove the shrimp to a plate and allow to cool off. Now combine all of the ingredients, including the rock shrimp, in a bowl. Stir everything gently together and it is ready to use.

ROASTED VINE-RIPE TOMATO AND GARLIC SAUCE FOR PASTA

From this simple and basic process you can build many different pasta sauces. This is such a great process for the tomatoes because it maintains their natural flavors while concentrating them even more.

Makes 6 to 8 servings

- 2 tablespoons olive oil
- 2½ pounds heirloom or other great quality vine-ripe tomatoes
- Pinch of kosher salt and fresh ground black pepper
- 5 Braised Garlic Cloves (see page 28)
- 2 tablespoons freshly snipped herbs (such as thyme, oregano, or basil)

Preheat oven to 400 degrees F. Coat the bottom of a large ovenproof cast-iron skillet with the olive oil and heat over medium heat. Cut the tomatoes in half; put in skillet and coat with the olive oil. Sprinkle the tomatoes with a pinch of salt and pepper. Put the skillet in the preheated oven for about 25 minutes. The tomatoes will roast and just caramelize a little around the edges. This will bring out and concentrate their flavor. The last 5 minutes add the braised garlic and finish roasting. The aroma of the tomatoes should now be filling your kitchen. Remove the skillet from the oven. When the tomatoes are cool enough to handle, carefully remove the skins. They should come right off. Now you have a beautiful skillet of oven-roasted tomatoes with garlic and olive oil.

For the most simple of sauces you can either hand-chop the ingredients for a more rustic feel or run the ingredients through a food processor for a more even-textured sauce. Whichever you do, get out the very last drop of the ingredients from the skillet because it is all flavor. Put the sauce back in the cast-iron skillet and simmer it over low heat for 5 minutes. Sprinkle in your favorite freshly snipped herb or herb mixture. You now have a great basic roasted tomato sauce to toss with your favorite pasta.

This amount of sauce works well with 1 pound of uncooked penne pasta. Simply cook the penne until it's al dente, drain off the water, and add it to the sauce, cooking on high heat for 1 minute so the sauce and the pasta come together. Serve the pasta in big bowls, sprinkled with more freshly snipped herbs and shaved Parmesan cheese.

Spicy Tomato-Orange Sauce with Kalamata Olives, Mozzarella, and Penne Pasta

This is a Mediterranean variation on Roasted Vine-Ripe Tomato and Garlic Sauce with Penne Pasta.

Makes 6 to 8 servings

1   recipe Roasted Vine-Ripe Tomato and Garlic Sauce (see page 113)

¼   teaspoon red chile flakes

Finely grated zest of 1 large orange

Juice of 1 large orange

1   pound penne pasta

1   pint multicolored heirloom cherry tomatoes

1   tablespoon olive oil

Pinch kosher salt and fresh ground black pepper

1   cup pitted kalamata olives

12   ounces fresh mozzarella, cut in ½-inch chunks

2   tablespoons freshly snipped basil

Fresh grated Parmesan cheese

To make this pasta, follow the directions for the Roasted Vine-Ripe Tomato and Garlic Sauce. Add the red chile flakes when you begin roasting the tomatoes. Add the orange zest and the orange juice after you have chopped the tomato mixture or have run it through the food processor, and then follow the recipe for the sauce to completion. While you are finishing the sauce, cook the penne in a big pot of boiling salted water. While the pasta is cooking, sauté the heirloom cherry tomatoes in a little olive oil with a pinch of kosher salt and fresh ground pepper. Sauté the tomatoes for about 5 minutes and they will cook just enough to bring out their flavor and have an appealing, warm texture. To finish the dish, when the pasta and the sauce are ready, add olives to the heated sauce. Add the drained pasta and the mozzarella to the sauce and cook on high heat for 1 minute until it all comes together. The mozzarella will begin melting. Serve the pasta in large bowls. Sprinkle with fresh basil, spoon the sautéed warm heirloom cherry tomatoes over the top, and for extra decadence add some fresh grated Parmesan cheese.

Paparadelli Pasta Bowl, New Orleans Style

This is untamed Southern pasta. It has all the basics we've been working on and then is taken to another level.

Makes 6 servings

1 recipe Roasted Vine-Ripe Tomato and Garlic Sauce (see page 113)

1 pound New Orleans smoked pork and crawfish sausage

1 pound uncooked paparadelli pasta

1 cup pitted kalamata olives

1 cup fresh baby spinach, washed and dried

12 ounces fresh ricotta cheese cut in 1-inch square chunks

1 pound mixed salad greens
   Balsamic Vinaigrette (see page 61)

12 ounces grated Parmesan cheese

To make this wild pasta, begin by making the Roasted Vine-Ripe Tomato and Garlic Sauce. Grill or roast the sausage for about 5 minutes and cut it into ½-inch-thick pieces. Set aside. Cook the paparadelli pasta in a large pot of boiling water until the pasta is al dente. While the pasta is cooking, add the sausage and the olives to the sauce and heat it up to a simmer in a large pot.

To finish the dish, drain the pasta and add it to the sauce. Turn the heat to high and gently stir the spinach and the ricotta cheese with a very light touch into the sauce and the paparadelli. You do not want the different elements to break down. Cook for 1 minute and then with a large serving spoon, spoon the pasta into six warmed pasta bowls. In the meantime, put the mixed salad greens into a hot sauté pan and give them a good squirt of Balsamic Vinaigrette; flash sear the greens for 1 minute. Serve 6 equal portions of the greens over each pasta bowl and sprinkle with the grated Parmesan cheese. Serve to your hungry guests and have a big glass of red wine immediately! I hope this works for you because it is fun, exciting, and delicious. Enjoy life!

brown sauce interlude

■■■■

My brown sauce is a concentrated concoction made from slow cooking vegetables, meat, spices, and herbs in water or meat stock and then distilling all the flavors of the ingredients into a reduced liquid that is used to make many of the sauces I use at the restaurant. This brown sauce can stand on its own as a great gravy, but as you will see, it is really the foundation, or mother sauce, of many great creations.

I love to make brown sauce. It embodies everything I think is great about cooking. The process feels good. It changes the atmosphere in the restaurant. There's an excitement in knowing how good it will taste, how smooth it will feel. Anticipating the warmth and depth of the broth comforting your body and your mind.

As I've grown up in cooking, I've realized that this brown sauce really started with my grandmother making a pot roast when I was a kid. She would brown her roast in a heavy cast-iron pot. Then she would add coarsely cut carrots, onions, celery, garlic, bay leaves, and pepper. She would then cover the ingredients with water and bring the pot up to a nice simmer. My mother would take it a bit further by adding red wine to the pot. The roast would slow-cook for hours. The house would fill up with the aromas of the simmering pot roast. It would make everyone feel good. When my dad came in from a hard day's work you could see him relax, see him come back alive.

Mom would then thicken the broth a little—it would be smooth and luscious. This was great home cooking. It also is the way that you make great brown sauce. She of course didn't know that. Didn't know you could take the broth and add it to reductions of wine and herbs and make a hundred different sauces. Those ladies, my mom and grandmother, were just doing some really good cooking. It got under my skin and stayed there.

Now, when I make brown sauce at the restaurant, my employees all gather around the kitchen counter at the end of the process when I'm about to strain the sauce. Well armed with fork and spoon, they dig in to the meltingly delicious vegetables (grandma's carrots, buttery onions, mushrooms) and pieces of meat, and they have a meal of it. My friend and sometime dishwasher Gustavo knows just what time of day I finish the brown sauce, and he mysteriously appears at the back door of the kitchen. I invite him in and he always helps the staff finish off the meal. Now I have a great foundation for my cooking, and my staff has a satisfaction that carries through the night. And Gustavo? He has a big Cheshire Cat smile on his broad face.

■ ■ ■ ■

Simple, Fast, and Delicious Homemade Brown Sauce: A Complete Guide

Makes 6 cups

2	tablespoons light olive or canola oil
2	medium-size onions, diced
4	carrots, peeled and cut in 1-inch chunks
6	cloves garlic, smashed
1	cup diced celery
½	cup chopped fresh parsley
¼	teaspoon dry whole-leaf thyme
⅛	teaspoon fresh ground black pepper
4	bay leaves
1	49-ounce can chicken stock
1	15-ounce can tomato sauce
6	tablespoons unsalted butter, melted
⅓	cup unbleached white flour
1	cup Madeira wine

It's best to use a medium-size, heavy-bottomed pot for this brown sauce. Add the oil to the pot and put over medium heat. Add the vegetables and cook until they are beginning to turn a nice golden color. Stir frequently. You are now bringing out all their flavor and character. Add the rest of the ingredients, except the Madeira, butter, and flour to the pot and bring the mixture to a boil. Turn the heat down and simmer the stock slowly for about 1½ hours. The stock should now have reduced down by about 25 percent and should taste pretty good. Now is the time to capture the flavors.

In a small saucepan, make a roux with the butter and flour. Cook the roux slowly over medium heat, stirring frequently until it is a beautiful reddish-brown color. Don't let it burn. Take your time. Add the roux to the stock. Turn off the heat under the stock first and then add the roux slowly. Be careful because it will splatter. Blend the roux thoroughly into the stock and put back over medium heat. Add the Madeira wine and heat up the sauce to a simmer; cook for about 15 minutes. When finished, the sauce will have a nice, slightly thickened viscosity and a shiny sheen and will taste delicious with a rich, concentrated flavor.

Let the brown sauce cool down some and then strain with two forks. Strain the sauce and

squeeze out all the juices from the vegetables. (Have a good snack with the strained vegetables.) You now have about 6 cups of delicious mother Brown Sauce that you can use to make gravies and many wonderful sauces. Here are a few to get you started.

Marchand de Vin: Sauté ¼ cup diced onion and 1 cup sliced mushrooms in 1 tablespoon olive oil for 3 minutes. Add 1 cup of a big bodied red wine, a pinch of dry oregano leaves, and a pinch of crushed black pepper and cook until the liquid reduces by one-third. Add 1 cup of Brown Sauce and cook until the sauce again reduces to a nice, slightly thickened shiny richness. Finish the sauce with a splash of brandy. Cook another minute and you are ready to serve it with a nice juicy steak for a quick little trip to New Orleans.

Piccata sauce: Sauté ½ cup sliced mushrooms in 2 teaspoons olive oil for 2 minutes. Add 1 cup of dry white wine, 1 tablespoon of fresh tarragon, and 1 teaspoon capers. Cook in a sauté pan until the mixture reduces by one-third. Now add 1 cup of Brown Sauce and a pinch of fresh ground black pepper and cook until the sauce again reduces to that perfect slightly thickened shiny richness. Not too thick and not too thin. Now finish off the sauce with a squeeze of

fresh lemon juice. Simmer again for 30 seconds. This goes great with country-fried pork chops, escalopes of veal, or sautéed chicken livers. For a creamy piccata sauce, simply add ½ cup cream to the finished sauce and cook until it again reduces to a nice creamy texture. Pour over sautéed chicken breasts and mashed potatoes and you will have a great meal.

Smothered gravy: Sauté ¼ cup diced onion and ½ cup sliced mushrooms in 1 tablespoon of butter for 3 minutes. Add 1 cup of Madeira, a pinch of coarse ground black pepper, and a teaspoon of fresh chopped rosemary leaves. Cook the mixture until it reduces by one-third and add 1 cup of Brown Sauce. Cook, again reducing by one-third. Add ½ cup heavy cream and cook the sauce until it becomes a beautiful gravy. Splash in a little brandy and cook a few more minutes. You now have a great smothered gravy for ground lamb Salisbury steaks, twice-baked potatoes, or really anything you can think of that sounds good with gravy.

This is old-fashioned cooking, the kind that gets into your soul. Try it. It works every time.

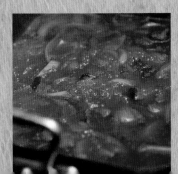

entrées

■■■■

Sheila and I arrived in Paris on a wet spring morning after taking the red-eye from New York. We ventured into the city on the Metro and came out onto the Saint Germain des Pres and set the first footprints of our lives on a Parisian boulevard. Through the fog of long-distance travel, all of the anticipation of coming to Paris exploded in us. We were actually here, in the heart of the world, where Hemingway and the Lost Generation found each other, where poets and rebels and thinkers and jazz musicians found a welcoming and intense community to sit around together in cafés over long nights and ponder the world and then hide away and write about it or make music about it or just make love. Here were the cafés and bistros they spent time in, the street markets and jazz bars, the exotic backstreets and the quays along the Seine where they searched for their lost idealism. It was a place of self-discovery, maybe of self-destruction so as to rebuild a new self. But most of all it was fun. Who do you want to be?

We found a beautiful small hotel on the Rue Jacob and secured a room for three nights. Then we walked the city and we ate the food. My favorite times were the mornings on the Rue Bucci at the street market, observing Parisian street life and drinking espresso at a sidewalk bar table, eating a chocolate croissant and fresh fruit. La petite dejeuner—breakfast in Paris. In the evening, walking the sidestreets to find the hidden bistro, with the golden light filtering out the front, we would go in and be struck by the energy of the place, the immediate greeting, the scurrying service people moving with intent to make sure everything was right, with the diners chattering away amid beautiful white linen-set tables in an atmosphere of stained glass, copper, ageless burnished wood, soft lights, and a relaxed intensity. And then the food. Traditional bistro fare, casual, inviting, and proud. It's what I gravitate to. The timelessness of the whole scene. The stamp of past generations that have lived their lives in and out of these bistros, and the coming generations that I hope will also.

We discovered many places and saw many sights in Paris that were like this, where the atmosphere, the people, and the food came together in an energy that was timeless, honest, and true. The experience was real, not scripted, and it got in your bones and you brought it home and you could see that our culture could use an infusion of it. At least I conceived that my restaurant could use some of it. So when I come to work that is the vision I bring with me to create my entrées. The energy of the backstreet Paris bistro, or a Bourbon Street bar, or a beach taco stand along the Sea of Cortez, or a funky Idaho steakhouse. We shoot for the realness we discovered and fell in love with on that trip to Paris, walking along the slick misty avenues, seeking out that one true experience.

■ ■ ■ ■

OLD-FASHIONED CRISPY-SKIN ROAST DUCKLING *with Wild Rice Toasted Pecan Pilaf and Baked Apple Brandy Compote*

This is a dish for the ages. The process comes from the ancient past—braising the main ingredient in a liquid with herbs, spices, and vegetables, rendering the meat of its fat, making it moist and juicy and developing amazing flavors and aromas. If done correctly it is one of the great ways to cook and eat. My roast duckling is without a doubt the most popular entrée at Vintage.

Makes 4 servings

Menu:

> Duckling
>
> Soy Balsamic Glaze
>
> Wild Rice Toasted Pecan Pilaf (see page 125)
>
> Baked Apple Brandy Compote (see page 126)
>
> Peppery Rosemary and Brandy Pan Juices (see page 126)

For the Duckling:

4   medium-size onions, peeled and sliced

4   carrots, peeled and diced

3   stalks celery, diced

½   bunch parsley, chopped

12   garlic cloves, smashed

6   bay leaves

1   tablespoon whole black peppercorns

2   (4- to 5-pound) ducklings*

     Water for the braising liquid

     Paprika for sprinkling

     Dry whole-leaf thyme for sprinkling

*Use Long Island–type ducks. They are available at your grocery store. They are nice and fat, which works better for the braising process. Don't use wild duck or Muscovy duck. They are not fat enough.

For the Soy Balsamic Glaze:

½   cup soy sauce

½   cup balsamic vinegar

⅓   cup Madeira wine

Preheat the oven to 415 degrees F. Place the vegetables, herbs, and peppercorns in the bottom of a 12- x 15- x 4-inch roasting pan. Remove the giblets from the duck cavity, rinse, and place on top of the vegetables. Rinse the ducks and place breast-down on top of the vegetables and giblets. Fill the roasting pan with water two-thirds up the sides of the ducks. Sprinkle the ducks with a thin coating of paprika and thyme.

Put the roasting pan on a stovetop burner and turn the heat on high. When the water begins to boil, remove the pan from the stove-top and place in the oven. Oven-braise the ducks for 1½ hours. Remove the pan from the oven and carefully turn the ducks over so they are breast-side-up in the roasting pan. Sprinkle each duck again with paprika and thyme. Add more water to the pan and return to the oven for another 30 minutes. After 30 minutes, reduce the heat to 325 degrees F and braise for 30 more minutes. The ducks should now be rendered of their fat and be tender and juicy. Remove them from the oven.

Carefully remove the ducks from the roasting pan and place them breast-down on a sheet pan. This is very important as it lets the juices run into the duck breasts. Now place the sheet pan into the refrigerator and cool the breasts down as fast as possible. When they are cold, you can wrap the ducks in clear plastic wrap and save them overnight to serve the next day.

While the ducks are cooling, strain the duck stock from the roasting pan. Let it chill overnight in the fridge; the duck fat will rise to the top and will harden so you can skim it off and discard it. You will be left with a delicious and pure duck stock. Reserve 1 tablespoon for the Wild Rice Toasted Pecan Pilaf. (You can also make this stock into a delicious brown sauce by following the instructions in the Brown Sauce Interlude chapter on page 118.)

When the ducks are absolutely cold, slice them in half right down the middle of the breast and the backbone. Slice off any protruding neck or tail pieces from each duck. Each duck half will be one serving. You are now ready to finish the dish.

Preheat the oven to 475 degrees F. Make the Soy Balsamic Glaze by mixing together the soy sauce and balsamic vinegar. About 20 minutes before you want to serve the duck, place 2 duck halves each, breast-side-out, into an ovenproof 10-inch sauté pan. Put Madeira in the pan with the ducks and drizzle the ducks with some Soy Balsamic Glaze. Put the ducks in the preheated oven for about 15 minutes. Check once or twice while baking. If the Madeira is running low add a little more—just enough to keep the pan moist. After about 15 minutes, remove the ducks from the oven. The skin should be a deep, rich color and be very crispy, but not burned. The flavor will be delicious and the meat moist and tender.

Remove the ducks from their pan to a cutting board. Slice halfway down between the breast and the leg and thigh. You now have two nice pieces for each serving. Place the breast and leg-thigh pieces side by side on a dinner plate in a pool of Peppery Rosemary and Brandy Pan Juices. Serve a scoop of Wild Rice Toasted Pecan Pilaf on one side of the plate and a large spoonful of Baked Apple Brandy Compote on the other side of the plate.

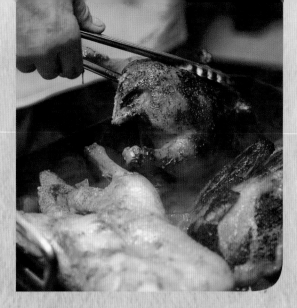

For the Wild Rice Toasted Pecan Pilaf:

1	tablespoon light olive oil
¼	cup diced onion
¼	cup diced celery
¼	cup chopped toasted pecans
2	cups cooked wild rice
	Pinch of salt and fresh ground black pepper
1	tablespoon reserved duck stock

To make the pilaf, heat oil in a medium sauté pan. When hot, add onion and celery and sauté 1 minute. Now add the pecans, wild rice, and a pinch of salt and pepper. Toss everything together and cook for about 2 minutes, tossing a few times. Add the duck stock and cover the pan. Turn heat to medium-low and let the pilaf rest a minute or two. It is now ready to serve.

For the Baked Apple Brandy Compote:

3   Granny Smith apples, peeled, cored, and cut in ½-inch wedges

¼   cup Madeira

¼   cup port

1½ tablespoons sugar

½   teaspoon ground cinnamon

3   tablespoons Bachelors' Berries with juice (see page 188)

You can make the compote ahead of time and finish it just before serving the duck. Put the apples in a medium-size, ovenproof sauté pan. Pour the Madeira and port over the top. Sprinkle with sugar and cinnamon and roast in the oven at 375 degrees F for 30 minutes. Now set aside until 10 minutes before serving.

To serve, add the Bachelors' Berries to the compote and reheat in the oven at the same time the duck is glazing. Remove when you take the duck out of the oven and serve.

For the Peppery Rosemary and Brandy Pan Juices:

½   cup Madeira

     Pinch crushed black peppercorns

1   teaspoon fresh rosemary leaves

½   cup Brown Sauce (see page 118)

1   tablespoon brandy

This is a simple and fast little process to do right after the duck comes out of the oven. After removing the duck from the pans, pour Madeira into one pan. Put on the stovetop and turn the heat up to high. Add crushed black peppercorns and rosemary leaves. Bring to a boil. Cook this for a minute or two, and then add Brown Sauce. Cook on high heat for 2 minutes and a beautiful sauce will form. During the last minute, add the brandy. Cook for 1 more minute and serve.

Seared Muscovy Drake Breast, Moroccan Style

Here are tastes from Morocco to Spain. Think of a Muscovy drake breast like you do a steak and cook it the way you like a steak. If you can't find the Muscovy drake breast, which is superior, normal duck breasts work just fine. Or substitute your favorite cut of steak in this recipe. This dish is about preparing all the elements and having them ready right when you want to serve the dish.

Makes 4 servings

Menu:

Red Wine Marinade

4   6-ounce Muscovy drake breasts, skin on

Couscous

Spinach and Goat Cheese Salad (see page 128)

Tomato Ginger Jam (see page 109)

For the Red Wine Marinade:

¾   cup dry red wine

3   tablespoons sherry vinegar

⅓   cup thinly sliced red onion

3   cloves garlic, smashed and minced

¼   teaspoon fresh ground black pepper

¼   teaspoon dry whole-leaf thyme

1   teaspoon freshly snipped rosemary

1   tablespoon freshly snipped oregano

1   teaspoon whole fennel seeds

1   tablespoon sugar

To make the marinade, simply mix up all the ingredients in a mixing bowl large enough to hold the duck breasts.

For the Duck:

Preheat oven to 450 degrees F. Score the skin of the duck breasts with three diagonal slices. Add the duck breasts to the marinade and leave them in at least 1 hour. When you take them out of the marinade, rub them with a little olive oil, a little kosher salt, and fresh ground black pepper. They are ready to cook.

For the Couscous:

2   cups water

1   tablespoon olive oil

¼   teaspoon kosher salt

1½   cups couscous

1   teaspoon lemon zest

¾   cup ¼-inch pieces zucchini

⅓   cup chopped sun-dried tomatoes

5   tablespoons almond slivers, toasted

1   tablespoon unsalted butter

To make the couscous, in a medium saucepan, bring the water, olive oil, and salt to a boil. Stir in the couscous, lemon zest, and zucchini. Bring back to a boil, cover with a tight lid, and remove from heat. Let it rest for 5 minutes. Gently stir in the sun-dried tomatoes and the almond slivers. Add the butter and let it rest for another 2 minutes. Fluff the couscous lightly with a fork and it is ready to serve.

For the Spinach and Goat Cheese Salad:

4   cups baby spinach leaves, washed and dried

¼   Spanish red onion, very thinly sliced

1   small orange, peeled, seeded, and cut into ¼-inch-thick wedges

20   teaspoon-size chunks of Montrachet goat cheese

1   teaspoon toasted sesame seeds

2   tablespoons freshly snipped mint leaves

6   tablespoons Sesame Mint Dressing (see page 56)

To make the salad, put all the ingredients, except the dressing, in order, in a medium salad bowl. Just before serving, add the dressing and toss the salad with a light touch. You do not want to beat it up. You want it nice and airy. It's ready to serve.

Now it's time to finish the dish. Start the couscous cooking. Have all the elements of the salad ready, and now you can pan sear the duck breast. Heat a 10-inch ovenproof sauté pan over high heat and get the pan fairly hot. Coat the bottom of the pan with a little olive oil. Place the breasts skin-side-down in the pan and sear them for about 5 minutes. If you think the pan is too hot, turn it down a little. Your goal is to get a nice sear in the duck breast skin. After about 5 minutes, simply put the pan in the oven. You do not need to turn the duck breasts over. They'll cook just fine. Cook them to your desired doneness. I like them rare to medium-rare. That takes about 5 minutes. Food cooks differently in every oven so be flexible and experiment a little with the time. Medium is okay, but if you cook them more than that they tend to dry out and get a little tough. When they have cooked to your desired doneness, remove from the oven and put skin-side-down on a cutting board. Let them rest a few minutes. While the breasts are resting, finish the couscous and toss the spinach salad.

Have four warm dinner plates ready. First slice the breasts on a diagonal about ¼ inch thick. Put a nice size scoop of the couscous on a section of each dinner plate. Fan the slices of duck breast beside the couscous on each plate. Pile, very lightly, one-fourth of the spinach salad by the couscous and the duck breast. Either serve a large tablespoonful of Tomato Ginger Jam right between the couscous and the duck or put the same portion of jam in a small ramekin and put it on the edge of the plate.

SEARED MUSCOVY DRAKE BREAST with Country-Style Baked Apples and Creamy Five-Rice Wild-Mushroom Risotto

I love the Muscovy breasts so much that I just had to do another dish with them. And here's a dish that works so well with cold smoking the meat. For the risotto, I use Lundberg's Wild Rice Blend because it is the best rice I have ever eaten. It contains long grain brown rice, sweet brown rice, wild rice bits, Wehani rice, and Black Japonica rice. It makes great risotto, rice pilaf, or just plain steamed rice. Ask your grocer to get you some. And no, I don't have stock in the company. I just think it's great stuff.

Makes 4 servings

Menu:

4   6-ounce Muscovy drake breasts, skin on

½   cup Vintage Basic Asian Marinade (see page 29)

4   Country-Style Baked Apples

Creamy Five-Rice Wild-Mushroom Risotto (see page 132)

To prepare the duck breasts, score the skin of each breast with three diagonal slices. Put the breasts in a bowl and coat them with the marinade. This marinade works fast and is very potent so leave the breasts in the marinade for only about 10 minutes. Now prepare the Little Chief Smoker. (If you don't have a smoker, use a BBQ or just don't smoke the breasts, but pan sear or charbroil them instead.) I like apple wood chips for duck. Cold smoke the breasts for about 40 minutes. This will infuse the meat with a great apple wood smoked flavor without cooking the meat. Remove the breasts from the smoker to a plate and put them in the refrigerator until you are ready to cook the dish.

For the Country-Style Baked Apples:

4   medium to small apples

½   cup sugar

½   teaspoon cinnamon

2   tablespoons brown sugar

2   tablespoons quick oatmeal

1   tablespoon all-purpose flour

2   tablespoons chopped toasted pecans

1   tablespoon dry Zante black currants

¼   teaspoon ground cinnamon

¼   cup unsalted butter, softened

1   cup Madeira wine

4   teaspoons brandy

Preheat oven to 375 degrees F. To make the baked apples, slice ¼ inch off the top of each apple. Core each apple two-thirds of the way through so you have a nice cavity in the apple to put the filling in. In a small bowl, mix together ½ cup sugar with ½ teaspoon cinnamon. Peel the top third of each apple and then dip apple in the bowl of cinnamon-sugar to coat the top third.

Crumble the remaining ingredients, except the Madeira and brandy, together in a bowl to make the filling. Fill each apple with a heaping amount of the crumble mixture. Place the apples in an 8-inch square Pyrex baking dish or an 8-inch sauté pan; pour in the Madeira and bake in the oven about 45 minutes. Five minutes before they are finished baking, pour 1 teaspoon of brandy over each apple. When they are finished baking, remove from the oven and set aside until you are ready to finish the dish. You can reheat them in the oven a few minutes before serving. By the way, these baked apples make a great dessert served warm with a scoop of Mountain Decadence Ice Cream (see pages 189 to 192) and a spoonful of Bachelors' Berries (see page 188).

For the Creamy Five-Rice Wild-Mushroom Risotto:

1   tablespoon light olive oil

1   cup mixed wild mushrooms, sliced in half (shiitake and crimini mushrooms are also good)

1½ cups dry Marsala wine

1½ cups Lundberg's Wild Rice Blend, cooked

1   teaspoon fresh rosemary leaves

¼   teaspoon fresh ground black pepper

1   cup Brown Sauce (see page 118)

½   cup heavy cream

    Splash brandy

1 tablespoon unsalted butter

Preheat oven to 450 degrees F. To make the risotto, heat up a 10-inch sauté pan with the olive oil. When it is hot, add the mushrooms and sauté them for about 5 minutes. Now add the Marsala wine, cooked rice, rosemary, and pepper and cook until the liquid reduces by about 25 percent. Add the Brown Sauce and bring to a high simmer; cook until it thickens a little bit and add the cream. Continue cooking until the sauce is silky and creamy but not heavy, about 5 minutes over medium heat. Now add the splash of brandy, simmer a minute, and turn off the heat. Add the butter and let the risotto rest.

To finish the dish, cook the duck breasts exactly as per the instructions for cooking the Moroccan Style Muscovy Drake Breasts (see page 128). When they have finished cooking, place the breasts on a cutting board skin-side-down and let them rest. While the duck breasts are cooking in the oven, reheat the baked apples in the same oven for about 10 minutes. When you are ready to serve the dish, give the risotto a shot of heat so it's nice and hot. To serve the dish, put a large scoop of the risotto in the center of each of four warmed dinner plates. Slice each duck breast on the diagonal into four or five slices and fan them over the risotto on each plate. Put one of the baked apples on each plate and drizzle a little of the pan juices from the apples over the duck slices. Serve the dish and enjoy.

SOUTHERN-STYLE BLACKENED FLATIRON STEAK *with Smoked Red Bell Pepper and Braised-Garlic Bruschetta and Marchand de Vin Sauce*

Inspired by New Orleans, the elements of this dish jump off the plate and say let's go party! So if you're feeling good, make this dish. The bruschetta alone makes a great appetizer or fun snack, and if you haven't used flatiron steak before you'll fall in love with it. It looks a little like flank steak but is a lot more tender. It's great to marinate; always thinly slice it on the diagonal when you serve it.

Makes 4 servings

Menu:

4	6-ounce pieces flatiron steak
¾	cup Red Wine Marinade (see page 127)
	Smoked Red Bell Pepper and Braised-Garlic Bruschetta
	Marchand de Vin Sauce (see page 134)

For the Steak:

Light olive oil

Vintage Spice Mix (see page 27)

Marinate the flatiron steak for 1 to 2 hours in the Red Wine Marinade. Remove the steak from the marinade, rub the meat with a light coating of olive oil, and sprinkle with the dry Vintage Spice Mix. It's your choice how much spice mix to use. The more spice mix the spicier and hotter the steak will be.

For the Smoked Red Bell Pepper and Braised-Garlic Bruschetta:

2	red bell peppers
12	Braised Garlic Cloves in Olive Oil (see page 28)
2	teaspoons capers

	Pinch kosher salt
	Pinch fresh ground black pepper
1	teaspoon brandy
1	tablespoon freshly squeezed lemon juice
1	tablespoon oil from the braised garlic
1	tablespoon each freshly snipped basil and oregano
8	¾-inch slices good quality baguette
	Balsamic Vinaigrette (see page 61)

To make the bruschetta, burn the skins of the red bell peppers on an open flame of a gas burner turned on high. Turn the peppers so that the whole pepper turns black. Put the peppers immediately in a bowl of cold water. When they have cooled down, peel off the blackened skin and you will have two nice skinless red bell peppers. Run the peppers under some cold running water to rinse off all of the blackened skin. Cut them in half, cut off the stems, and remove the seeds. Smoke the bell pepper halves on a wire rack in a cold smoker. I like the Little Chief brand. The peppers will absorb smoke fast, so smoke

Vintage

133

them for only about 10 minutes. Use a mild wood like apple wood. When the peppers are finished smoking, remove them to a cutting board and cut each half into four strips. Place the strips in a small bowl. Cut the 12 braised garlic cloves in half and put them in the bowl with the peppers. Add the capers, salt, pepper, brandy, lemon juice, and tablespoon of garlicky oil and toss together. Now toss in the fresh herbs. Set aside. Lightly brush each baguette slice with a little olive oil. Set aside.

For the Marchand de Vin Sauce:

2 tablespoons light olive oil

⅓ cup diced red onion

2 Braised Garlic Cloves (see page 28), mashed and diced

1 cup sliced crimini mushrooms

1 cup sliced shiitake mushrooms

1 cup full-bodied red wine

¼ teaspoon dry leaf oregano

¼ teaspoon fresh ground black pepper

1 cup Brown Sauce (see page 118)

1 tablespoon brandy

You can make the sauce ahead of time and reheat to serve. Heat up a 10-inch sauté pan with the oil. When the pan is medium-hot, add the diced onion, garlic, and mushrooms and sauté them for about 5 or 6 minutes. Add the red wine, oregano, and pepper and bring to a hearty simmer for 3 minutes. Add the Brown Sauce; bring the sauce back to a hearty simmer and cook until the mixture reduces to a beautiful red wine mushroom sauce that is not too thick and not too thin. Finish the sauce with the brandy and simmer a few more minutes. Now let's finish the dish.

Preheat oven to 425 degrees F. Traditionally, blackening is done in a very hot sauté pan or iron skillet, but I like to do it on a very hot spot on my charbroiler. Flatiron steak is best served rare or medium-rare. Medium is okay, but cooked more than that and it tends to lose quality. For a rare steak, cook the flatiron for about 4 minutes on each side. While the steaks are cooking, finish the Marchand de Vin. Warm it back up for a minute or two before serving, add a little more brandy, and cook the sauce for 1 minute. It's ready to serve.

When you start cooking the steaks, put the red bell pepper relish in an ovenproof sauté pan and put it in the oven to warm up. When you turn the steaks over, put the baguette slices on a cooler section of the broiler and let them grill for about 2 minutes per side. Don't burn them. You want them nicely crispy on the outside and warm and soft on the inside. When the steaks have finished cooking, remove them to a cutting board and let them rest for about 2 minutes. Remove the warmed red bell pepper relish from the oven.

To serve the dish, spoon the Marchand de Vin onto the center of each of four warm dinner plates. Slice each steak on the diagonal into 4 slices and fan the steak over the sauce. Place 2 slices of the grilled bread on each plate and drizzle some Balsamic Vinaigrette (see page 61) over each slice so it soaks in a little. Don't use too much Balsamic Vinaigrette. Spoon a dollop of the warmed red bell pepper relish onto each slice of grilled bread. I like to sprinkle the plate with a little thinly sliced green onion and freshly snipped oregano. Then serve.

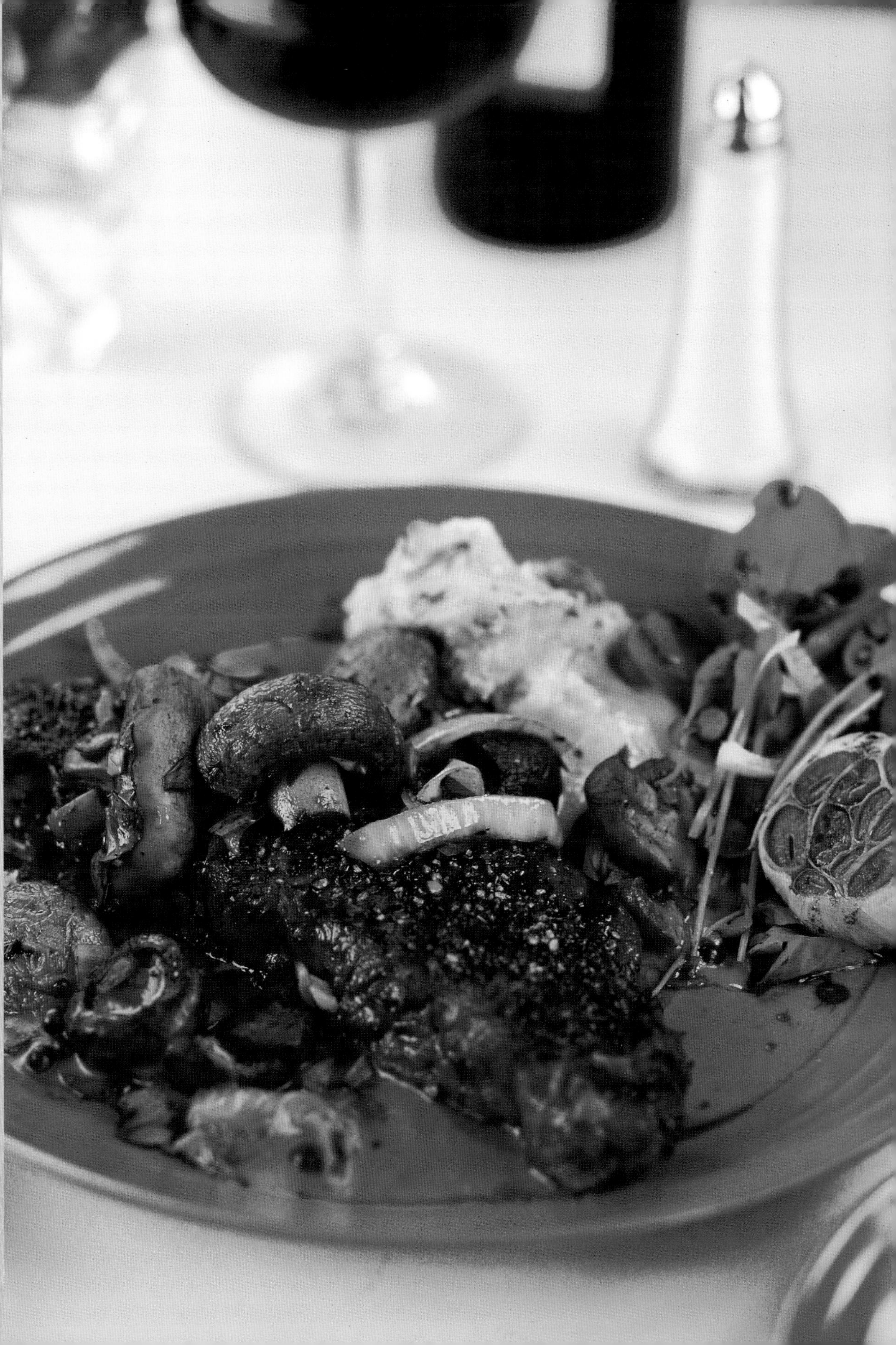

CLASSIC PARIS BISTRO PEPPER STEAK (BACKSTREET VERSION)

In my mind this is the quintessential bistro pepper steak. All of these elements put together with this steak speak to me of a rainy night in Paris. I can feel the cold, but the thought of the vibrant bistro and the luscious dish warms me to the bone.

Makes 4 servings

Menu:

4   10-ounce New York steaks

Baked Yukon Gold Gorgonzola Smashed Potatoes

4   Slow-Roasted Garlic Bulbs (see page 138)

Grilled Warm Balsamic Mushroom and Sweet Red Onion Relish (see page 138)

Green Peppercorn Brandy Cream Pan Gravy (see page 138)

1   bunch fresh watercress, divided into 4 smaller bunches for garnish

Balsamic Vinaigrette (see page 61)

For the Steaks:

1   tablespoon coarse crushed black pepper

Press the crushed peppercorns into the top surface of each steak. If you really like lots of crushed pepper, feel free to use more. You can do this right before you cook the steaks or ahead of time and keep the steaks in the fridge until you are ready to cook.

For the Baked Yukon Gold Gorgonzola Smashed Potatoes:

5   medium-size Yukon Gold potatoes, quartered, skin on

6   tablespoons unsalted butter

¼   teaspoon kosher salt

¼   teaspoon fresh ground black pepper

1   tablespoon diced fresh parsley

2   tablespoons thinly sliced green onions

½   cup grated Parmesan cheese

6   tablespoons cream

8   1-inch square chunks of Gorgonzola cheese

Preheat oven to 350 degrees F. To make the smashers, cover the potatoes with water in a medium-size pot. Bring to a boil and cook until they are fork-tender. Drain the potatoes into a colander when they are done and then put them back in the same pot they cooked in. Add 4 tablespoons of the butter, salt, pepper, parsley, green onions, Parmesan cheese, and cream. With a potato masher, smash everything coarsely together. Check for seasonings; adjust if necessary. Spoon the mixture into a lightly oiled 6-inch teflon-coated sauté pan. Dot the potatoes with small pieces of the remaining butter and press the chunks of Gorgonzola cheese in to the surface of the potatoes. Drizzle a little more cream over the top. You can now hold this pan of smashers until about 25 minutes before you serve the steaks, at which time you should bake the smashers in the oven.

For the Slow-Roasted Garlic Bulbs:

4   Whole garlic bulbs

    Olive oil

    Sprinkling kosher salt

    Sprinkling fresh ground black Pepper

Preheat oven to 275 degrees F. Use small- to medium-size garlic bulbs. With a French knife, slice the top ¼ inch off of each garlic bulb. Rub the garlic bulbs with a generous amount of olive oil and sprinkle with a little kosher salt and pepper. Put the bulbs in a 6-inch ovenproof sauté pan. Cover the pan with tinfoil, crimping down the sides, and roast the garlic for about 45 minutes to 1 hour in the oven. When done, the garlic should be soft, sweet, and buttery. Set aside to rewarm just before serving the dish.

For the Grilled Warm Balsamic Mushroom and Sweet Red Onion Relish:

2½ tablespoons olive oil

4   ¼-inch-thick slices of sweet Italian red onion

16 medium-size crimini mushrooms

1   tablespoon freshly snipped basil

1   tablespoon thinly sliced green onion

    Pinch kosher salt

    Pinch fresh ground black pepper

    Balsamic Vinaigrette (see page 61)

To make the relish, paint a little olive oil on each side of the red onion slices. Cut the mushrooms in half, put them in a mixing bowl, and toss with 1½ tablespoons of the olive oil. (Wait to cook the relish until the steaks are cooking so it can be hot and fresh when you serve it. You can have all the ingredients ready up to that point.)

Spread out the mushrooms on a medium-hot charbroiler along with the onion slices and grill them for about 2 minutes. Turn them over and grill for 2 more minutes. Remove the mushrooms to the mixing bowl. Remove the onion slices to a cutting board and slice them in halves or quarters. Put the onions in the bowl with the mushrooms. Add the snipped basil, green onion, and pinch of salt and pepper. Now drizzle in about 2 tablespoons of Balsamic Vinaigrette and toss the relish.

For the Green Peppercorn Brandy Cream Pan Gravy:

I	cup Madeira wine
I	tablespoon drained whole green peppercorns
I	pinch coarse crushed black peppercorns
¼	teaspoon freshly snipped tarragon leaves
I	cup Brown Sauce (see page 118)
½	cup cream
2	tablespoons brandy
I	tablespoon unsalted butter

To make the sauce, add the Madeira to a 10-inch sauté pan along with the green peppercorns, crushed black peppercorns, and tarragon. Turn the heat on high and reduce the liquid by one-third. Stir in the Brown Sauce and cook until it reduces by one-third. Add the cream and cook the sauce until it reduces to a perfect silken viscosity that coats a spoon but is not too thick. Add the brandy and cook for 2 minutes. It should be perfect. Turn off the heat and drop in the butter; let it melt while stirring it in.

You are ready to finish the dish. Have the charbroiler set to a medium-high temperature. Have the smashers in the oven warming up so the Gorgonzola melts into the potatoes. Start grilling the steaks to your desired doneness and finish the mushroom red onion relish as per the instructions. Give the sauce a last flash of heat. Warm up the whole roasted garlic in the oven. To serve the dish, have four warm dinner plates ready. Place one steak on the left side of each plate with the meaty edge of the New York facing out and the fatty edge to the inside of the plate. Put a nice dollop of smashers in the right center portion of the plate. Spoon some sauce over each steak and let it spread around the potatoes. Spoon one-fourth of the mushroom relish over each steak. Place one-fourth bunch of watercress on the right side of the plate just below the smashers and give it a squirt of Balsamic Vinaigrette. Put the roasted garlic bulb right at the base of the watercress.

The dish is now ready to serve. I hope it makes you feel like that rainy night in Paris, coming into the warmth and comfort of a friendly place.

Tenderloin of Beef, Parisian Brasserie Style (Upscale Version)

I had fois gras for the first time when Sheila and I went to Paris in the spring of 1991. Scott Mason, fellow chef and restaurant owner of the Ketchum Grill, said that while in Paris we must have dinner at Brasserie Julien in the Montmarte district. He said it would be like going to another planet. He was right. With stained-glass ceilings, beautiful lighting, huge mirrors, people crammed at tables like sardines, and great food, it was like a wild 1920s psychedelic dream. I'll never forget our night there. So here's to Brasserie Julien and my first experience with fois gras.

Makes 4 servings

Menu:

Roasted Garlic Potato Gratin

Beet Caviar

Fresh Rosemary and Brandy Pan Sauce
(see page 141)

Pan-Seared Mushrooms (see page 141)

4   1-ounce slices of Fois Gras

4   6-ounce tenderloin of beef filets

For the Roasted Garlic Potato Gratin:

1   whole roasted garlic bulb

1½ pounds Idaho baking potatoes, peeled, rinsed, and dried off

1¼ cups cream

1   cup freshly grated Parmesan cheese

Pinch kosher salt

Pinch fresh ground black pepper

1½ tablespoons unsalted butter

Preheat oven to 300 degrees F. To make the gratin, first roast the garlic bulb. Coat the bulb with a little olive oil, wrap it in tinfoil, and roast it in the oven for about 30 to 40 minutes, until the garlic is soft and squeezable. Slice the potatoes thinly and put them in a mixing bowl. Squeeze out the garlic cloves from the roasted bulb and put them in the bowl. Add the cream, half of the Parmesan cheese, and the salt and pepper. Mix the ingredients together gently. Grease a 7-inch round cast-iron skillet with some of the butter and then pour in the potato mixture. Arrange the potatoes neatly and shake the skillet gently so everything settles nicely. Sprinkle the remaining Parmesan over the top of the gratin and dot with the remaining butter. Turn the oven up to 350 degrees F and bake until the potatoes are tender, about 40 minutes.

For the Beet Caviar:

2   medium-size beets with stems removed, thoroughly rinsed and dried

1   tablespoon olive oil

1 to 2 tablespoons Balsamic Vinaigrette (see page 61)

Pinch kosher salt

Pinch fresh ground black pepper

Preheat oven to 350 degrees F. Coat the beets with the olive oil, put them in an ovenproof skillet or sauté pan, cover the pan with tinfoil, and roast for about 1 hour or until the beets are tender inside. Check on their progress from time to time. Remove them from the oven and let them cool off enough to handle. Peel the skin off the beets, cut them into coarse pieces, and then put them in a food processor. Add 1 tablespoon Balsamic Vinaigrette and the salt and pepper, and pulse. When the beets begin to have the texture of caviar, stop pulsing. They should be bright and shiny and moist. If they are a little dry, add a little more Balsamic Vinaigrette. Store the Beet Caviar in a bowl and rewarm just before serving.

For the Fresh Rosemary and Brandy Pan Sauce:

- 1 cup Madeira wine
- 20 fresh rosemary leaves
  Pinch fresh coarse ground black pepper
- 1 cup Brown Sauce (see page 118)
- 2 tablespoons brandy

Simmer the first four ingredients in a saucepan until they reduce by half. Add the brandy and simmer about 2 more minutes.

For the Pan-Seared Mushrooms:

- 1 tablespoon olive oil
- ¾ cup fresh morel mushrooms
- ¾ cup shiitake mushrooms
  Pinch kosher salt and fresh ground black pepper
- 1 tablespoon balsamic soy glaze (½ balsamic vinegar mixed with ½ soy sauce by volume)

Heat up a 10-inch sauté pan with the olive oil. When it's hot, throw in the mushrooms with the salt and pepper and sear them for about 2 minutes, tossing them so they sear on all sides. Toss in the balsamic soy glaze and toss the mushrooms again to coat. Do this just before serving the dish.

For the Fois Gras:

Simply cut four 1-ounce slices of fois gras and set aside. You can substitute a good pâté slice if you can't get the fois gras.

For the Steaks:

  Olive oil
  Fresh rosemary

To put the dish together, rub the tenderloins with a little olive oil and fresh rosemary and sear them on the charbroiler. Cook them for about 3 minutes a turn, turning them 4 times. While they are cooking, reheat the gratin. Reheat the beet caviar by placing 4 tablespoons of the caviar in a ramekin and warming it in the oven. Flash sear the mushrooms and finish the pan sauce. When you've turned the tenderloins for the final time, place a slice of the fois gras on top of each tenderloin. Have four warm dinner plates ready. Ladle ¼ cup of the pan sauce onto each plate. Place a tenderloin into the left center of the sauce. Put a nice serving of the gratin next to each tenderloin. Put a tablespoon dollop of beet caviar next to the fois gras on top of the tenderloin. Now sprinkle one-fourth of the mushrooms and any pan drippings around each tenderloin. Serve the dish. Leftover gratin is great the next day.

Idaho Rib-Eye Steak Feast

Up in the high country of Idaho we like to eat hearty. We are also lucky enough to have local sources of all of the products I use in this dish. The beef is raised right here in the Wood River Valley. The tomatoes come from what I call the Provence of Idaho—Hagerman, a magical agricultural area along the Snake River, 60 miles from my home. The potatoes are, of course, Idaho bakers. And the morel mushrooms we pick ourselves in the hills around our valley after a good rain. So this dish truly is an Idaho Steak Feast.

Makes 4 servings

Menu:

4   servings Idaho Twice-Baked Potatoes

20   Oven-Roasted Mushrooms (see page 144)

Rosemary Brandy Pan Juices (see page 144)

4   10-ounce rib-eye steaks rubbed with a little olive oil and fresh rosemary

Tricolored Vine-Ripe Tomato Salad (see page 105)

For the Idaho Twice-Baked Potatoes:

2   large Idaho russet potatoes, washed and scrubbed

2   tablespoons unsalted butter, cut into small pieces

2   tablespoons thinly sliced green onions

2   tablespoons sour cream

1   cup grated medium-sharp cheddar cheese

¼   cup cream cheese, cut into small pieces

Kosher salt and fresh ground black pepper to taste

Preheat oven to 400 degrees F. To make the twice-baked potatoes, pierce the tops of the potatoes with a fork a few times and then bake them in the oven for about 1 hour or until they are tender. Let the potatoes cool a few minutes and then cut them in half lengthwise. Scoop out the potato centers into a bowl, being careful not to tear the potato skins. Add the butter, green onions, sour cream, and half of the cheddar cheese to the bowl. Mash the ingredients together with a light touch and season with a pinch of salt and pepper. Gently fold in the cream cheese. Refill the potato skins with the mashed potato mixture and sprinkle them with the remaining cheddar cheese. To reheat the potatoes place them on a baking sheet and put in the oven at 400 degrees F 15 minutes before you serve the feast.

For the Oven-Roasted Mushrooms:

    Mushrooms

    Olive oil

    Pinch kosher salt

    Pinch fresh coarse ground black pepper

¼   teaspoon dry whole-leaf thyme

Set an oven to 400 degrees F. For this dish I use the morel mushrooms we pick locally, but any type of mushroom will work. Shiitake or crimini are especially good. To roast the mushrooms, toss them in a bowl with a little olive oil, a pinch of kosher salt, a pinch of fresh coarse ground black pepper, and the thyme. Put the mushrooms on a baking sheet and roast in the oven for about 12 minutes. Put the mushrooms in the oven 3 minutes after you put in the twice-baked potatoes for both to finish at the same time.

For the Rosemary Brandy Pan Juices:

1   cup Madeira wine

    Pinch fresh coarse ground black pepper

2   sprigs fresh rosemary

½   cup Brown Sauce (see page 118)

2   tablespoons brandy

To make the pan juices, heat the Madeira in a sauté pan with the pepper and rosemary sprigs on high heat until the liquid reduces by half. Stir in the Brown Sauce and continue to cook over high heat until the liquid reduces by one-fourth. Pour in the brandy and cook on high heat for 2 minutes. It is ready.

To finish the Idaho Rib-Eye Steak Feast, put the twice-baked potatoes in the oven to reheat 15 minutes before serving. Have your broiler set on medium-high. Put the prepared mushrooms in the oven to roast. Start broiling the steaks. Cook steaks to desired doneness, about 10 minutes for medium-rare. To serve the dish, put ¼ cup of the pan juices on each of four warm dinner plates. Put a finished rib-eye on the left portion of the plate with the meat edge facing out. Put a twice-baked potato to the upper right side of the steak. Serve the tomato salad in the lower right portion of the plate, stacking the tomatoes about four levels high. Then sprinkle each steak with the roasted mushrooms. Serve it while it's hot.

NATURALLY RAISED VEAL RACK CHOPS, CREAMY PICCATA STYLE

Veal with lemon caper sauce is a match made in heaven. I care about how products are raised and produced, and there is some controversy about veal production. I agree with those who are uncomfortable about veal production in darkened barns in small isolated cages. I will not buy any veal raised under those conditions under any circumstance. The veal we use at Vintage is raised outside with their mothers, free-range style. It's a better form of production and one to be supported and encouraged.

Makes 4 servings

4   1-inch-thick veal rack chops with bone in (ask your butcher if he can get them)

¼   cup Vintage Basic Asian Marinade (see page 29)

1   tablespoon olive oil

2   tablespoons unsalted butter

28   medium-size shiitake mushrooms

2   cups Madeira wine

1   tablespoon fresh tarragon leaves

⅛   teaspoon fresh ground black pepper

2   teaspoons drained capers

1½   cups Brown Sauce (see page 118)

1   tablespoon freshly squeezed lemon juice

½   cup heavy cream

1   tablespoon brandy

I love to coat these veal chops with a little Vintage Basic Asian Marinade. It adds a nice flavor to the veal. For even more flavor, cold smoke the chops for about ½ hour in a Little Chief Smoker with hickory wood chips. The chops are great this way. Really, you don't even need a sauce with this method. Marinate the chops, and smoke them if you like, or just rub them with the olive oil and a little salt and pepper. Then grill them to your desired doneness. Serve them with some sautéed mushrooms and Parmesan Smashed Potatoes (use the recipe for Gorgonzola Smashed Potatoes on page 137, but eliminate the Gorgonzola) and you have a great dish.

For the sauce, melt the unsalted butter in a 12-inch sauté pan. When the butter is hot, but not burning, add the mushrooms and sauté for about 5 minutes. Add the Madeira, tarragon, pepper, and capers and cook on high heat until the liquid reduces by half. Add the Brown Sauce and continue cooking until the liquid reduces by about one-fourth. Add the lemon juice and cook for 2 minutes. Add the cream and cook until the sauce reduces to a beautiful silky viscosity that is not too thick or too thin. Add the brandy and cook for 1 minute.

To serve the veal chops, put a chop on a warm dinner plate and spoon the sauce and some mushrooms over the top. I recommend serving the veal with Parmesan Smashed Potatoes and buttery green beans. Just steam or boil the beans till tender, drain, and sauté with a little unsalted butter and a pinch of kosher salt. You'll like the combination.

Smoked Pork Tenderloin, Wine Country Style

Pork tenderloin, hickory wood smoke, red and green grapes, wild rice and toasted pecans, tawny port. You cannot go wrong with these ingredients in a dish. So let's get right to it!

Makes 4 servings

Menu:

2   12-ounce pork tenderloins

½   cup Vintage Basic Asian Marinade (see page 29)

Wild Rice, Toasted Pecan, and Sweet Corn Fritters

Honey-Roasted Red and Green Grapes (see page 148)

Tawny-Port Pan Sauce (see page 148)

For the Pork:

Marinate the 2 pork tenderloins in a bowl with Vintage Basic Asian Marinade. Turn it a few times so it is covered evenly. Prepare the Little Chief Smoker with hickory wood chips and cold smoke the pork for about 45 minutes. This can be done ahead of time. Take the pork out of the smoker and store in the refrigerator until you are ready to cook. (If you don't have a cold smoker, you can eliminate this step.)

For the Wild Rice, Toasted Pecan, and Sweet Corn Fritters:

2   medium eggs

⅓   cup cream

Pinch kosher salt

Pinch coarse fresh ground black pepper

2   teaspoons white all-purpose flour

2   tablespoons thinly sliced green onions

⅓   cup chopped toasted pecans

⅓   cup fresh sweet corn kernels (frozen sweet corn is okay to substitute)

1¼   cups wild rice, cooked

Make the fritters while the pork is cooking on the charbroiler. To make the fritters, in a mixing bowl beat the eggs with the cream, salt and pepper, flour, and green onions. Now stir in the chopped pecans, corn kernels, and wild rice.

Heat up a 12-inch sauté pan with a little light olive oil to medium-hot. Don't let the oil smoke. Make eight dollar-size fritters with the batter. Treat them just like pancakes. Cook them for about 4 minutes on each side. The fritters should be crispy on the outside and cooked through but moist and steamy on the inside.

For the Honey-Roasted Red and Green Grapes:

1   cup seedless red grapes

1   cup seedless green grapes

2   tablespoons honey

2   tablespoons brandy

Preheat oven to 400 degrees F. Ten minutes before you are ready to serve the pork, put the grapes in an 8-inch ovenproof sauté pan. Drizzle the honey over the grapes and pour in the brandy. Put the pan in the oven for 10 minutes; the grapes will roast in the honey and brandy and make delicious pan juices. Don't overcook the grapes. You want them to be hot and the juices to be bubbly.

For the Tawny-Port Pan Sauce:

1   cup tawny port

    Pinch fresh ground black pepper

½   cup Brown Sauce (see page 118)

Simmer the port and the pepper in a small saucepan until the liquid reduces by half. Add the Brown Sauce and continue simmering until the sauce coats a spoon but is not too thick. You can make this sauce ahead of time and reheat it just before serving. Add a little more port to the pan when you reheat the sauce.

To put the dish together, grill the pork tenderloins on a charbroiler set to medium-hot. You don't need to cook them too fast. It will take about 15 minutes to cook them to medium. For medium-rare, the cooking time will be less. Play with the time until you get the meat just the way you like it. Remove the tenderloins to a cutting board when finished cooking and let them rest for a few minutes.

While the pork is cooking, reheat the sauce, put the grapes in the oven, and make the fritters.

To serve the dish, slice each pork tenderloin on the diagonal into eight equal slices. Drizzle each of four warm dinner plates with the Tawny-Port Pan Sauce. Fan out 4 pieces of pork tenderloin onto each plate. Place 2 fritters to the side of the pork servings and sprinkle each plate with an equal amount of grapes and their pan juices.

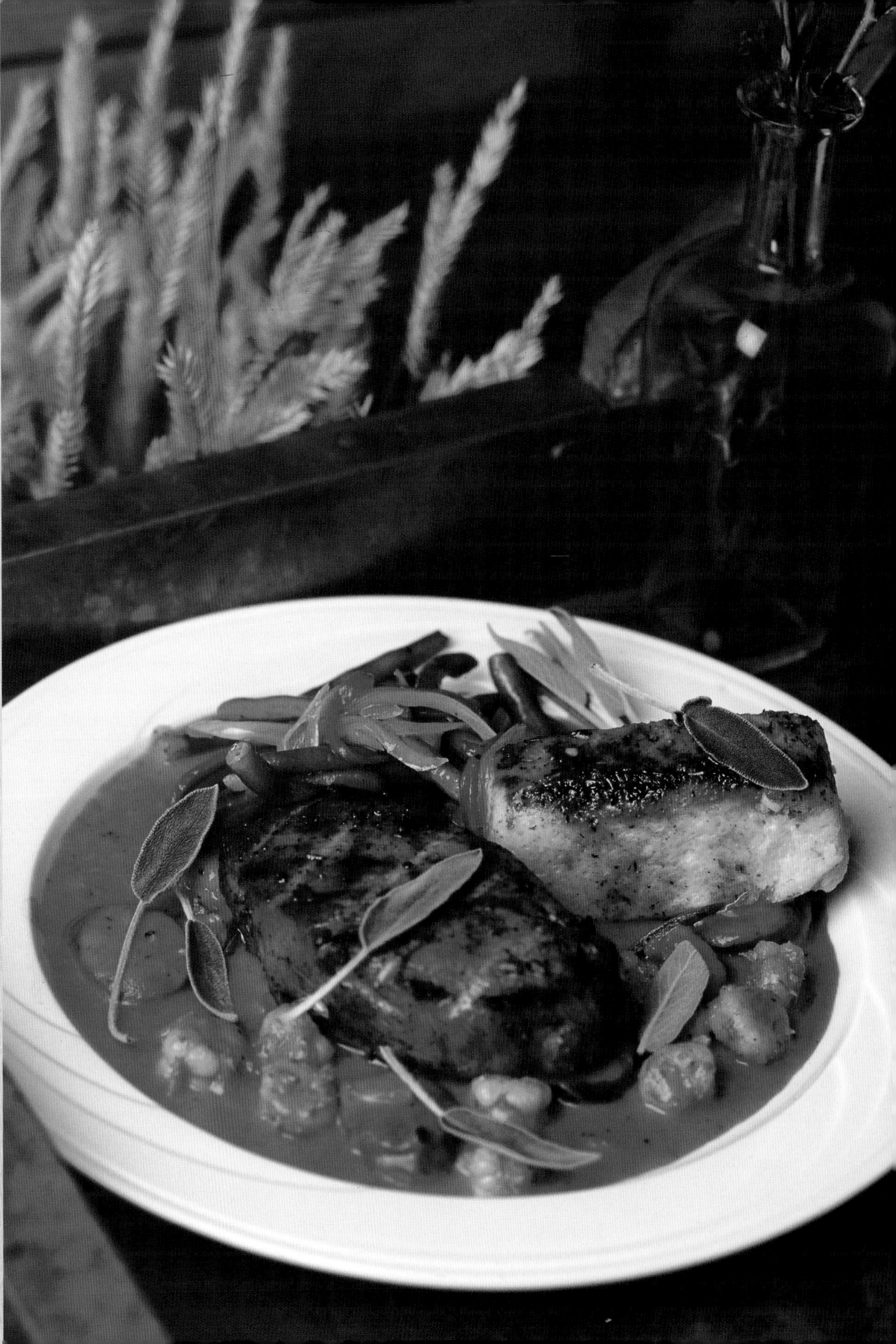

SPICY PORK LOIN CHOP with Sweet Corn and Cheddar Cheese Polenta and Rock Shrimp, Fresh Sage, and Smoked Pork Sausage Gravy

I love the freedom of Southern cooking where you can make gravies with shrimp and smoky sausages, and serve them with spicy pork or fish. Add some cheesy polenta and a big scoop of slaw and you have a veritable feast that explodes with flavor. It's all about flavor down there, and loving life. Here's a dish with that spirit.

Makes 4 servings

Menu:

4   double-cut pork loin chops

Sweet Corn and Cheddar Cheese Polenta

Rock Shrimp, Fresh Sage, and Smoked Pork Sausage Gravy (see page 152)

For the Chops:

⅓   cup Vintage Basic Asian Marinade (see page 29)

1   tablespoon Vintage Spice Mix (see page 27)

Marinate the chops in the Vintage Basic Asian Marinade for 15 minutes. The sweet and spicy marinade goes great with the Vintage Spice Mix. If you want to add another layer of flavor, cold smoke the chops in the Little Chief Smoker for about 30 minutes. When you are ready to cook the chops, coat them on all sides with the Vintage Spice Mix.

For the Sweet Corn and Cheddar Cheese Polenta:

3   cups water

Pinch kosher salt

Pinch fresh ground black pepper

¾   cup fresh or frozen sweet corn kernels

¾   cup polenta

2   tablespoons unsalted butter

1   cup medium-sharp grated cheddar cheese

Olive oil

Sprinkling of chile powder

To make the polenta, bring the water to a boil in a medium saucepan. Add the salt, pepper, and corn kernels. Stirring the mixture with a wooden spoon, slowly add the polenta. Turn the heat down so the mixture is at a high simmer. Cook the mixture and stir it often so it does not stick to the bottom of the pan or get lumpy. As the polenta begins to thicken, add the butter and keep stirring. After a few more minutes add the grated cheddar cheese and stir it in. Turn the heat down and continue to stir and cook the polenta. You will feel it blossom. It opens up and softens and becomes really creamy and delicious. Be patient, as this process will take 20 to 30 minutes. The polenta is done when it is thick and creamy. Pour it into a 5- x 9-inch bread pan that has been rubbed with a little olive oil and sprinkled with a light coating of chile powder. Cover the surface with a piece of clear plastic wrap and put it in the refrigerator to set. Give it about 2 to 3 hours to set up. When the polenta has set up all the way through, you can unmold it onto a plate. It is now ready to cut into individual serving portions.

For the Rock Shrimp, Fresh Sage, and Smoked Pork Sausage Gravy:

1½ tablespoons light olive oil

½ medium yellow onion, peeled and thinly sliced

1 cup Cajun smoked pork sausage, cut in thin slices

2 cups Madeira wine

12 fresh sage leaves, cut in half

Pinch fresh ground black pepper

1½ cups Brown Sauce (see page 118)

¾ cup uncooked rock shrimp, lightly sprinkled with Vintage Spice Mix (see page 27)

½ cup heavy cream

2 tablespoons bourbon

To make the gravy, heat up the olive oil in a 10-inch sauté pan and add the onion and sausage slices. Cook over medium heat for 3 to 4 minutes and then add the Madeira, sage leaves, and pepper. Cook on high heat until the liquid reduces by almost half. Add the Brown Sauce and cook on a high simmer until the sauce begins to thicken. Cook for 2 more minutes and then add the rock shrimp and the cream. Continue to cook at a high simmer until the sauce reduces to the perfect viscosity for gravy.

It should not be too thick or too thin, but should have a nice body. Add the bourbon and cook on high for 2 minutes. The sausage gravy should be spicy, tasty, and delicious.

To finish the dish, slice the polenta into 1-inch-thick slices. Either pan sear or charbroil the pork loin chops. They will need to cook about 12 to 15 minutes depending on how well done you want them. Give them 4 turns during the cooking process so they cook through evenly. I like them best cooked medium to medium-rare.

While the chops are cooking, heat up a large Teflon-coated sauté pan with a light coating of olive oil. Add the polenta slices and sear each side for about 3 minutes. Finish the gravy while the chops are cooking. Give the sauce a final blast of heat just as the chops are finishing. To serve the dish, place a chop on each of four warmed dinner plates, put a slice of polenta beside each chop, and in equal portions ladle over the gravy. If you serve a large dollop of Spicy New Orleans Slaw (see page 77) with each plate, the dish will be perfect.

APPLE WOOD–SMOKED PORK LOIN CHOP

with Gorgonzola Polenta, Caramelized Yams, and Black Mission Fig, Ginger, and Port Sauce

Here's another combination of ingredients that go great with pork. I like the way the figs and the ginger complement and contrast with the Gorgonzola, the yam, and the port.

Makes 4 servings

Menu:

4   double-cut pork loin chops

⅓   cup Vintage Basic Asian Marinade (see page 29)

    Gorgonzola Polenta

    Caramelized Yams

    Black Mission Fig, Ginger, and Port Sauce (see page 154)

For the Pork Chops:

Marinate the chops in the Vintage Basic Asian Marinade for 20 minutes. Start up the Little Chief Smoker with apple wood chips and cold smoke the chops for 30 to 45 minutes. Set them on a plate covered with clear plastic wrap in the refrigerator until you are ready to cook them.

For the Gorgonzola Polenta:

Follow the recipe for cooking the Sweet Corn and Cheddar Cheese Polenta (see page 151), but leave out the corn and the cheddar cheese and add ¾ cup Gorgonzola cheese crumbles. Lightly oil ten 3-ounce demitasse espresso cups. When you are finished cooking the polenta, pour it into each of the demitasse cups. These make a perfect molded serving size for the polenta. You'll have more than you need for the pork chops but that's okay. Have some with scrambled eggs for breakfast.

For the Caramelized Yams:

2   medium-size yams

⅓   cup sugar

1   tablespoon ground cinnamon

Preheat oven to 350 degrees F. Wash the yams and pierce them with a fork a few times. Bake them for about 1 hour or until they are cooked through. Let them cool down. Mix together sugar and cinnamon in a pie tin. When you are ready to cook the pork, cut the yams into four 1½-inch-thick slices. Put them face down in the cinnamon-sugar mixture for 5 minutes and then sear them, (sugar-side-down) in a 10-inch sauté pan in hot butter. Cook until the sugar caramelizes but does not burn. Turn the yams over and heat in the oven with the polenta.

For the Black Mission Fig, Ginger, and Port Sauce:

24   sun-dried black mission figs, cut in half

2   cups ruby port, divided

2   tablespoons thin matchstick-cut fresh ginger

   Pinch fresh ground black pepper

1   cup Brown Sauce (see page 118)

2   tablespoons brandy

Put the halved figs in a bowl, cover with 1 cup of the ruby port, and let marinate overnight. To make the sauce, put the figs and their marinating juices, plus an additional 1 cup of port, into a 10-inch sauté pan along with the ginger matchsticks and the pepper. Cook over high heat until the liquid reduces almost by half. Add the Brown Sauce and, on a high simmer, cook the sauce until it thickens enough to have a beautiful rich purple luster but is not thick or cloying. Add the brandy and simmer on high for 2 minutes. Reheat just before serving the dish.

To finish the dish, heat oven to 400 degrees F. The chops are best cooked on a charbroiler or BBQ. They will take about 12 to 15 minutes to cook, turning them four times for even cooking. They are best cooked medium-rare to medium, but cook them how you like them. While the chops are cooking, put four of the demitasse polenta cups in the oven. They will take about 8 to 10 minutes to heat through. Caramelize the yams as instructed and put them in the oven. Give the sauce a final blast of heat. To plate the food, unmold the polenta onto each plate, holding the hot demitasse cup with a towel. The hot polenta will come right out of the cup with a little shake. Place a yam, caramelized-side-up, beside the polenta. Place a chop beside the polenta and serve an equal portion of the sauce over each chop.

SUN VALLEY PECAN-CRUSTED CHICKEN

This is a dish that I've been serving up here for twenty years. Our guests will not let me take it off the menu. And why should I? It's a great dish, with flavor, texture and balance. The Tomato and Black Currant Chutney recipe (see page 108) tells the story of how this dish came to be.

Makes 4 servings

Menu:

Tomato and Black Currant Chutney (see page 108)

Pecan Saltine Cracker Crumbs

Sour Cream Mustard Sauce

Dijon-Mustard Butter Rub

4   5-ounce boneless and skinless chicken breasts

To make Sun Valley Pecan-Crusted Chicken, first make the Tomato and Black Currant Chutney well ahead of time to allow it to cool off. Then prepare the Pecan Saltine Cracker Crumbs, the Sour Cream–Mustard Sauce, and the Dijon-Mustard Butter Rub.

For the Pecan Saltine Cracker Crumbs:

1½ cups coarsely ground pecans

1½ cups ground saltine crackers

Mix the ground pecans and saltine crackers in a medium-size bowl. Set aside.

For the Sour Cream Mustard Sauce:

1½ cups sour cream

2   tablespoons Dijon mustard

Blend well in a small bowl and set aside.

For the Dijon-Mustard Butter Rub:

½   cup unsalted butter

2   tablespoons Dijon mustard

Melt the butter in a small saucepan or in a microwave-safe bowl and blend in the mustard.

For the Chicken:

To make the chicken, lightly pound each breast to about ⅜ inch thick. Take each chicken breast and coat one side with a painting of the mustard butter. Put that breast, mustard-butter-side-down, in the saltine cracker crumb mixture. Give it a firm press so the crumbs adhere. Repeat for the other side. Do this to all of the chicken breasts and put them on a platter until you are ready to cook.

Preheat oven to 450 degrees F. To cook the chicken, melt 3 tablespoons unsalted butter in a 12-inch sauté pan. When the butter is hot, add the chicken breasts. Cook them for about 3 minutes. They should be turning a nice, crispy medium brown color. Turn them over and cook for 3 more minutes. Remove the chicken breasts to a baking sheet, saving the crumbs that remain in the sauté pan. Put the baking sheet in the oven and cook the breasts for about 5 more minutes. While the chicken is cooking, add 8 tablespoons of the Sour Cream Mustard Sauce to the sauté pan that the chicken cooked in; blend the crumbs and juices from the chicken with the sour cream mixture. Just before the chicken is done cooking, heat up the sauce until it is just bubbly. Don't keep cooking it. Take the chicken out of the oven and place 1 breast on each of four warmed dinner plates. To one side of each breast, add a 2-tablespoon dollop of the chutney. To the other side of the breast, pour over 2 or 3 tablespoons of the warm Sour Cream Mustard Sauce. Serve this dish with some light lemony vegetables and you will have a great dinner.

Asian Mahogany Chicken Bowl

I like the style of cooking that features hot and cold contrasts with variations in textures and flavors that are crispy, crunchy, tender, and juicy. This dish has it all in an Asian style. The Asian Mahogany Chicken Bowl is all about preparing the ingredients ahead of time and putting the dish together at the last minute.

Makes 4 servings

Menu:

Mahogany Marinade

4   7-ounce plump chicken breasts, skin on

Nuoc Cham Drizzle (see page 160)

Asian Green Salad (see page 160)

1½ cups uncooked Chinese egg noodles

½   cup fresh basil leaves

½   cup green onions, thinly sliced on the diagonal

1   cup honey-roasted peanuts

For the Mahogany Marinade:

1   cup Vintage Basic Asian Marinade (see page 29)

½   teaspoon fresh ground star anise seed

2   tablespoons thinly sliced green onions

1   tablespoon lightly toasted sesame seeds

¾   cup hoisin sauce

2   teaspoons Asian black vinegar (or you can substitute balsamic vinegar)

1   tablespoon honey

Mix all the ingredients for the marinade together in a bowl. Reserve ½ cup of the marinade to use later as a drizzle over the noodles. Rinse and pat dry the chicken breasts and put them in the remaining marinade for about 30 minutes. Start up the Little Chief Smoker using apple wood chips. Cold smoke the breasts for 45 minutes. (If you don't have a cold smoker, you can eliminate this step.) When finished, remove the breasts to a plate and hold in the refrigerator until you are ready to cook the breasts.

For the Nuoc Cham Drizzle:

- 1 clove garlic, smashed and minced
- 1 red or green jalapeño chile pepper, minced
- ¾ teaspoon sambal chili paste
- ¼ cup sugar
- ⅔ cup hot water
- ¼ cup Asian fish sauce (you can find this in the Asian section of most supermarkets)
- 2 tablespoons freshly squeezed lime juice
- 2 tablespoons very thinly sliced matchstick carrots
- 2 tablespoons thinly sliced green onions

To make the Nuoc Cham, add the first four ingredients to a mixing bowl. Pour in the hot water and dissolve the sugar. Add the rest of the ingredients. Store in the refrigerator.

For the Asian Green Salad:

- 3 cups thinly sliced bok choy
- 3 cups thinly sliced Chinese cabbage
- 1 small cucumber, peeled, cut in half length-wise, seeded, and thinly sliced
- 1 red bell pepper, cut in half, stemmed, seeded, and thinly sliced
- ½ red onion, peeled and thinly sliced across the grain
- ⅓ cup fresh mint leaves, sliced
- ⅓ cup fresh basil leaves, sliced

Toss the salad ingredients and hold in refrigerator until ready to serve.

Preheat oven to 425 degrees F. Bring a large pot of water to a boil for the noodles.

To cook the smoked chicken breasts, in a hot 12-inch ovenproof sauté pan with a very light coating of oil, sear the breasts skin-side-down for 2 minutes. Turn them over and then put the pan in the oven. The breasts will take about 10 minutes to cook through depending on how thick they are. You want them tender and juicy.

Start the noodles in the boiling water. The noodles and the chicken breasts should get done about the same time. When the breasts are done cooking, put them on a cutting board to rest for a few minutes. Drain the noodles into a colander in the sink.

To serve the dish, have four large pasta bowls at room temperature. Put one-fourth of the Asian Green Salad in the bottom of each bowl. Drizzle each salad with Nuoc Cham. With a pasta serving fork, put a nice serving of the hot drained noodles over each salad and drizzle the noodles with the reserved Mahogany Marinade. Slice the chicken breasts across the grain into 4 or 5 slices per breast and fan them over the noodles. Drizzle the pan juices from the sauté pan over each breast. Sprinkle the fresh basil, green onions, and honey-roasted peanuts over each bowl and serve.

Idaho-Raised Rack of Lamb, English Pub Style

England sometimes gets a bad rap about the quality of its food. It's pretty good actually and I especially like the traditional and regional fare found in pubs all over the country. In that spirit I make this dish, especially in winter, where in England the chill goes to the bone. We use Idaho mountain-raised lamb for its full and delicious flavor and to support our local agriculture.

Makes 4 to 5 servings

Menu:

Old English Savory Bread Pudding

Honey-Ale Roasted-Shallot Pan Sauce (see page 164)

2   14-ounce Idaho-raised lamb racks

4   sprigs fresh rosemary for garnish

For the Old English Savory Bread Pudding:

¾   cup small cubes country white sourdough bread

1¾   cups milk

2   whole eggs plus 1 egg yolk

2   tablespoons molasses

1   tablespoon coarsely chopped fresh sage

½   teaspoon dry whole-leaf thyme

2   tablespoons dry Zante black currants

½   teaspoon fresh ground black pepper

Pinch kosher salt

2   tablespoons unsalted butter, melted

Preheat oven to 375 degrees F. To make the bread pudding, put the bread in a bowl and add the milk. Let the bread soak up all the milk and then crumble up the mixture. In another bowl, beat the eggs and egg yolk with the molasses and then mix in the rest of the ingredients except the salt and butter. Thoroughly mix the bread and milk mixture with the egg and molasses mixture. Lightly butter four to five 6-ounce Pyrex cups and fill them with the bread pudding mixture. Put the cups in a large baking dish and fill it with water about two-thirds up the sides of the Pyrex cups. Bake the bread puddings for about 45 minutes to 1 hour. They should be puffed up and firm to the touch when they are done. Remove them from the water bath and you can serve them immediately or let them cool down and warm them up later when you need them.

For the Honey-Ale Roasted-Shallot Pan Sauce:

1 tablespoon unsalted butter

12 whole shallots, peeled

1 12-ounce bottle dark brown ale

Pinch fresh ground black pepper

1 teaspoon fresh rosemary leaves

1 tablespoon honey

1¼ cups Brown Sauce (see page 118)

2 tablespoons brandy

Preheat an oven to 350 degrees F. First, melt the butter in an 8-inch ovenproof sauté pan. Add the shallots and coat with butter. Put them in the oven to roast for 20 minutes. Remove. In a 10-inch sauté pan, put the dark ale, roasted shallots, pepper, rosemary, and honey and cook over high heat until it reduces by about one-third. Add the Brown Sauce and continue cooking on high heat until the sauce reduces to a perfect silky viscosity. Not too thick or too thin. Add the brandy and cook for 2 more minutes. The sauce should be ready. Just reheat before serving.

For the Lamb:

3 tablespoons unsalted butter, melted

2 tablespoons Sun Valley Honey Mustard (other honey mustard may be substituted)

1 tablespoon chopped parsley

1 cup ground bread crumbs

Preheat oven to 450 degrees F. In a small saucepan or in a microwave-safe bowl, melt the butter and mix it with the Sun Valley Honey Mustard. In a separate bowl, mix the chopped parsley with the bread crumbs. Sear the whole lamb racks either on a charbroiler or in a large sauté pan. Sear the lamb for 4 minutes on each side. Take the racks off the heat and coat tops and sides with the mustard butter. Sprinkle on the bread crumb mixture, making sure the crumbs stick to the racks. Put the racks in a large sauté pan, crumb-side-up, and roast in the oven until done, about 10 to 12 minutes for medium-rare. The timing on getting lamb to the proper doneness is a learning experience, so experiment with the time. When the lamb is done, remove it to a cutting board and let it rest for a few minutes so the juices can settle and the meat will be more supple when you slice it.

While the racks are cooking, finish the sauce so it is hot when you serve the dish. Reheat the bread puddings by putting them in the hot oven directly on the oven rack for about 7 minutes. Now the dish can be served. Have four warmed dinner plates ready. Unmold each bread pudding by holding the cup with a towel and running a butter knife around the edge of the bread pudding. It will pop right out onto the dinner plate. Slice each lamb rack into 8 chops and fan out 4 chops onto each plate. Spoon the Honey-Ale Roasted-Shallot Pan Sauce over the lamb. Garnish the plate with a nice sprig of fresh rosemary and serve the dish.

Butterflied Leg of Lamb, Southwestern-France Style

Butterflying leg of lamb is a way of trimming the lamb leg into individual portions that you can then cook like a steak. It's a great alternative to cooking the leg as a whole piece. I like to grill or BBQ the butterflied leg and then serve it thinly sliced. This is a favorite dish of mine because I love Grilled Ratatouille, which goes well with lamb. I recommend that you have your butcher butterfly the lamb leg and then you can use it over a number of meals. How about a slow-cooked lamb stew with the rest? We use Idaho lamb when available, but lamb from the other western states is quite good also.

Makes 4 servings

Menu:

4   6-ounce pieces butterflied leg of lamb
     Grilled Ratatouille
     Provencal Pan Sauce (see page 166)
     Grilled Bread with Golden Heirloom
     Tomatoes (see page 166)

For the Butterflied Leg of Lamb:

½   cup Red Wine Marinade (see page 127) or
     Vintage Basic Asian Marinade (see page 29)

Marinate the lamb. If you are using the Red Wine Marinade, marinate for 1 hour. If you are using the Vintage Basic Asian Marinade, marinate for 15 minutes. Set lamb aside until you are ready to cook.

For the Grilled Ratatouille:

4   ¼-inch-thick slices red onion, lightly
     brushed with olive oil on both sides

16   medium-size shiitake mushrooms, tossed
     with 2 tablespoons of olive oil

2   medium-size red bell peppers, cut in half,
     stemmed, seeded, and cut into ½-inch
     strips

6   ⅜-inch-thick slices eggplant, lightly brushed
     with olive oil on both sides

2   tablespoons freshly snipped basil leaves
     Kosher salt and fresh ground black pepper
     to taste

2 to 3 tablespoons Balsamic Vinaigrette
     (see page 61)

Prepare the ingredients for the ratatouille ahead of time and then 5 minutes before serving the dish, grill all the vegetables on a charbroiler. Remove them to a mixing bowl. Add the basil, salt, and pepper and toss everything gently in the Balsamic Vinaigrette. It is ready to serve. The Grilled Ratatouille also makes a great salad served over mixed greens.

For the Provencal Pan Sauce:

- 1   teaspoon fresh rosemary leaves
- 1   shallot, diced
- 4   shiitake mushrooms, diced
- 1   tablespoon olive oil
- 1¼ cups red wine from the Rhone Valley of France

    Pinch coarse ground black pepper
- 1   cup Brown Sauce (see page 118)
- 2   tablespoons brandy

Make the sauce by sautéing the rosemary, shallot, and mushrooms in the olive oil for 3 minutes. Then add the red wine and the pepper. Cook at a high simmer until the liquid reduces by one-third. Add the Brown Sauce. Simmer until the sauce reduces to the perfect silky sheen, not too thick or too thin. It is all about feel, so use your instinct to get the feel when the sauce is ready. If it is too thick, add a little more wine and simmer a minute more. If it is too thin, keep cooking until it has that unmistakable luster of a great sauce. Add the brandy and simmer for 2 more minutes. Serve, or warm it back up with a splash of brandy when you are ready to serve the dish.

For the Grilled Bread with Golden Heirloom Tomatoes:

    4 or 8 ½-inch-thick slices of a good baguette (either 1 or 2 per serving)

    Olive oil

    Vintage Basic Vinaigrette (see page 59)
- 2   ¼-inch-thick slices tomato for each bread slice
- 1   tablespoon freshly snipped basil

Make the grilled bread 5 minutes before you serve the dish. Brush both sides of the bread slices with a little olive oil. Put them on a grill for 2 minutes per side. Give each of the bread slices a squirt of the Vintage Basic Vinaigrette. Place them on the side of four warm dinner plates, lay 2 tomato slices on each piece of bread, drizzle on a little more of the vinaigrette, and sprinkle the tomatoes with the snipped basil.

To cook the lamb and finish the dish, grill the lamb on a charbroiler for about 10 to 12 minutes, turning the lamb four times. Again, it's all about touch, feel, and timing, so with experience you will learn exactly when the meat is done to your preference. When done, remove the lamb to a cutting board and let it rest for a few minutes. Meanwhile, finish the Grilled Ratatouille, reheat the sauce, and finish the grilled bread. To plate the dish, slice each piece of lamb across the grain into four equal slices. Ladle some sauce onto each plate and fan out the lamb over the sauce next to the grilled bread and tomatoes. Spoon equal portions of the Grilled Ratatouille over the lamb.

IDAHO GROUND-LAMB SALISBURY STEAK
with Smothered Mushroom and Sweet Onion Gravy

I call this dish extreme comfort food. It is great to serve when the weather is getting cold and appetites are getting hearty. If you haven't already, you'll fall in love with ground lamb. It is so tasty. It makes great burgers or meatballs, with fennel seed and ground pepper, to go with a tomato sauce for pasta. If these 8-ounce lamb Salisburys are just too big for you, make them smaller and you'll have more servings.

Makes 4 servings

For the Ground-Lamb Salisbury Steaks:

1¾ pounds ground Idaho lamb (other ground lamb may be substituted)

¾ cup diced sweet onion

¼ teaspoon plus a pinch fresh ground black pepper

¼ teaspoon plus a pinch kosher salt

3 tablespoons of your favorite smoky BBQ sauce

Smothered Mushroom and Sweet Onion Gravy

Put the ground lamb in a large mixing bowl and add the remaining ingredients. Mix everything together by hand until it is evenly blended. Form the mixture into four equal-size oblong patties that are about ¾ inch thick. Put them on a platter until you are ready to cook them.

For the Smothered Mushroom and Sweet Onion Gravy:

2 tablespoons unsalted butter

1 cup coarse chopped sweet onion (a red Italian, Walla Walla, or Vidalia)

24 medium-size mixed mushrooms (domestic button, crimini, and shiitake work well), cut in half

1½ cups Madeira wine

1 tablespoon diced fresh tarragon leaves

⅛ teaspoon coarse ground black pepper

1¼ cups Brown Sauce (see page 118)

¾ cup heavy cream

2 tablespoons brandy

Make the smothered gravy by melting the butter in a 12-inch sauté pan. Add the onions and mushrooms when the butter is hot and sauté for about 4 minutes. You want to bring out the flavors of the onions and mushrooms. Stir the ingredients a few times so they cook evenly. Add the Madeira, tarragon, and pepper and cook on high heat until the liquid reduces by one-third. Add the Brown Sauce and cook the gravy until it thickens to a nice silky viscosity. Add the heavy cream and cook until the sauce turns into a beautiful smothered gravy, not too thick and not too thin. Add the brandy and cook for 2 more minutes. You can make the gravy while the Salisburys are cooking.

Cook the Salisbury steaks in one of three ways. One way is to cook them on a hot griddle or in a cast-iron skillet. The griddle or skillet should be hot enough to turn the steaks a nice browned color but not burn them. Turn them four times for even cooking. Cook about 10 minutes for medium-rare or more or less to taste. You can cut into a portion of the steak to see exactly how much it is cooked. Feel free to learn by experimenting. A second way to cook the steaks is on a charbroiler or grill. The timing is about the same. The last way to cook them is on a George Foreman Grill. They work perfectly well for this kind of food, and in the winter when your BBQ is put away, it's a great way to grill.

Serve the steaks on four warm dinner plates smothered with the gravy. I love to serve the Salisburys with smashed potatoes. Try the Gorgonzola Smashed Potatoes (see page 137) or Parmesan Smashed Potatoes (use the recipe for Gorgonzola Smashed Potatoes, but eliminate the Gorgonzola). Another variation of the smashers is to press roasted or braised garlic cloves into them when you reheat them before serving. The garlic adds an earthy sweet garlicky richness to the potatoes that is delicious.

Fresh Ahi Tuna Steak *with Provencal Spring Salad,*
Deviled Eggs, and Horseradish Sour Cream Drizzle

The salad, with its inspiration from southwestern France, can stand alone. With a piece of quickly grilled ahi tuna and deviled eggs it becomes a great meal.

Makes 4 servings

Menu:

Provencal Spring Salad

Deviled Eggs

Horseradish Sour Cream Drizzle
(see page 172)

4   6-ounce fresh ahi tuna steaks

For the Provencal Spring Salad:

6   small new red potatoes, boiled until fork-tender

8   spears fresh spring asparagus, steamed for 2 minutes, then cooled

¼   pound baby green beans, steamed until just tender, then cooled

3   tablespoons slivered Braised Garlic Cloves (see page 28)

3   medium vine-ripe tomatoes, cut into 6 wedges each

1   small red bell pepper, cut in half, stemmed seeded, and cut lengthwise into ⅛-inch-wide strips

1   small yellow bell pepper, cut in half, stemmed, seeded, and cut lengthwise into ⅛-inch-wide strips

1   tablespoon drained capers

16   pitted nicoise or kalamata olives

12   fresh and crisp basil leaves

⅓   cup Vintage Basic Vinaigrette (see page 59)

1   tablespoon Dijon mustard

To make the salad, prep all the vegetables. Arrange them in a large salad bowl. Mix the mustard with the vinaigrette and then pour it over the salad and toss very gently. Let the salad marinate for ½ hour before serving.

For the Deviled Eggs:

6   hard-boiled eggs

2   tablespoons mayonnaise

1   tablespoon imported Dijon mustard

1   teaspoon sour cream

½   teaspoon prepared horseradish

1   teaspoon chopped fresh French tarragon

Pinch kosher salt

1   teaspoon mild New Mexico red chile powder

Peel the eggs. Make sure all shell fragments are removed. Cut the eggs in half lengthwise; remove the yolks to a bowl and set the whites on a plate. Add the rest of the ingredients, except the red chile powder, to the bowl and mash everything together until it is well blended and smooth. Spoon the deviled mixture back into the egg white halves. Lightly sprinkle each deviled egg with a little red chile powder. Serve the eggs slightly chilled when you serve the dish.

For the Horseradish Sour Cream Drizzle:

¼   cup sour cream

1   tablespoon mayonnaise

1   teaspoon prepared horseradish

1   tablespoon half-and-half

2   teaspoons freshly squeezed lemon juice

4   turns of ground pepper from the pepper grinder

Mix all the ingredients in a small bowl. Blend to a smooth cream. If it is too thick to drizzle, add a few drops of water to thin it a little.

For the Tuna Steaks:

4   teaspoons Peppery Orange Aioli (see page 27)

1   teaspoon Vintage Spice Mix (see page 27)

To finish the dish, spread ½ teaspoon of the Peppery Orange Aioli over the top portion of each ahi steak. This will prevent the ahi from sticking to the grill and will also impart a nice flavor. Start cooking the ahi, aioli-side-down, on a medium-hot charbroiler. After the ahi cooks for 1½ minutes, give each steak a quarter turn so you get nice grill marks on the fish. Spread the remaining aioli on the top portion of the ahi and sprinkle with the Vintage Spice Mix. Cook for 1 more minute, then turn the fish over and cook the other side for 2 minutes. I like my ahi seared rare, so if you want it done more, cook it longer. But be careful because ahi cooks fast and gets very dry if it's overcooked.

To serve the dish, put an equal portion of the salad on each of four dinner plates. Put an ahi steak just off center over the salad. Arrange 3 deviled egg halves around each plate and drizzle the mark of Zorro over the dish using the Horseradish Sour Cream Drizzle!

Fresh Mahimahi, South Pacific Style

Sheila and I were married in the fall of 1982. We went to Hawaii for our honeymoon to the island of Maui. I've never forgotten the macadamia nut–crusted mahimahi I had there in a famous restaurant of the era. I've forgotten the name of the restaurant but not the taste of the fish. I've been doing my own varying versions of the dish ever since. This is one of them.

Makes 4 servings

Menu:

Macadamia Nut Coconut Crust

4   5-ounce pieces mahimahi

Wild Rice and Bean Sprout Egg Foo Yung

Tropical Mango, Jicama, and Pineapple Slaw (see page 76)

Golden Plum, Hoisin, Sesame Drizzle (see page 174)

For the Macadamia Nut Coconut Crust:

1   cup coarsely ground, lightly toasted macadamia nuts

1   cup ground saltine cracker crumbs

1   cup unsweetened shredded coconut

3   tablespoons unsalted butter, melted

1   tablespoon Sun Valley Honey Mustard (you can substitute any honey mustard)

Mix the first three ingredients together in a mixing bowl. In another bowl, mix together the warm melted butter with the honey mustard. Lightly coat each piece of mahimahi with the honey mustard butter and then dip the pieces in the macadamia nut mixture to completely coat each piece of fish. Put the crusted mahimahi on a plate until you are ready to cook.

For the Wild Rice and Bean Sprout Egg Foo Yung:

3   eggs

3   tablespoons heavy cream

1   cup Lundberg's Wild Rice Blend, cooked (you can substitute a long grain brown rice if you can't find the rice blend)

1   cup bean sprouts

2   green onions, thinly sliced

2   tablespoons freshly snipped basil

⅛   teaspoon kosher salt

⅛   teaspoon fresh ground black pepper

To make the egg foo yung mixture, in a mixing bowl beat the eggs with the cream and then fold in the remaining ingredients. Fry the egg foo yung about 6 minutes before the dish is to be served. In two 10-inch lightly oiled sauté pans over medium-high heat, make eight equal-size egg foo yung patties. Treat them like pancakes and cook them for about 3 minutes per side. They should be crispy on the outside and hot and steamy on the inside. Serve two per serving.

For the Golden Plum, Hoisin, Sesame Drizzle:

1   cup Vintage Basic Asian Marinade (see page 29)

2   tablespoons Asian Golden Plum Sauce (available in the Asian section of most supermarkets)

1   tablespoon hoisin sauce

1   tablespoon Asian black vinegar (or substitute balsamic vinegar)

1   green onion, thinly sliced

1   tablespoon lightly toasted sesame seeds

1   teaspoon freshly squeezed lime juice

Make the drizzle by mixing all the ingredients together in a small mixing bowl. Set aside until ready to serve.

To cook the dish, preheat oven to 425 degrees F. Melt 1 tablespoon of unsalted butter with 2 tablespoons of light olive oil in a 12-inch ovenproof sauté pan. When the pan is medium-hot, add the fish and cook for about 3 minutes. The nut crust should turn a nice medium golden brown. Turn the fish over and then put the sauté pan in the oven for about 5 minutes. This should cook the fish through but leave it nice and juicy.

Meanwhile, fry the egg foo yung so that the fish and the egg foo yung get done at the same time.

To serve the dish, drizzle the Golden Plum, Hoisin, Sesame Drizzle in a circular motion around each of four warm dinner plates. Lay down two of the egg foo yung overlapping each other on the left side of the plate. Spoon a nice big mound of the slaw on the upper right side of the plate. Place the crusted mahimahi up against the egg foo yung and the mound of slaw. I like to garnish the dish with long fresh-cut chives that I call a chive checkerboard. Serve the dish and enjoy.

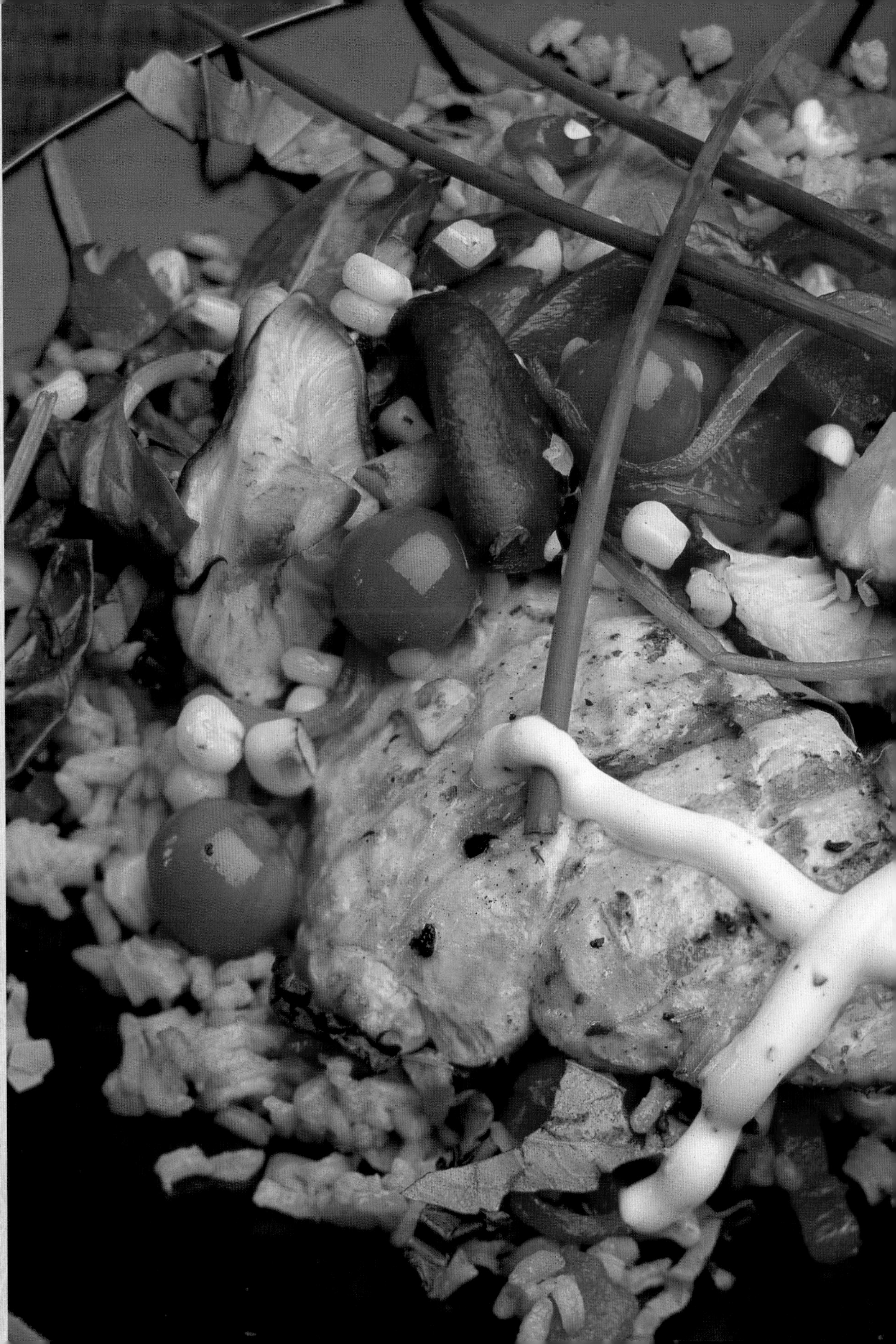

CHARBROILED FRESH TROLL KING SALMON, OLD-CALIFORNIA STYLE

This dish has a natural comforting quality. I guess it's just that the chemistry of the ingredients have an appealing healthy aura surrounding them. I find salmon to be the ultimate comfort-food fish, and with Spanish Rice and the pan roast of vegetables, comforting it is.

Makes 4 servings

Menu:

Spanish Rice

Vegetable Pan Roast

4   6-ounce fillets wild king salmon

For the Spanish Rice:

2¼ cups chicken stock or water

1   cup long grain white rice, uncooked

2   tablespoons unsalted butter

¼   teaspoon kosher salt

    Pinch saffron threads

¼   teaspoon ground toasted cumin seed

½   teaspoon mild New Mexico chile powder

½   cup diced red bell pepper

1   teaspoon finely grated lemon zest

Put all the ingredients for the Spanish Rice in a saucepan. Stir everything together and bring to a boil. Cover the pan tightly and reduce heat to low. Cook for 20 minutes or until all the liquid has been absorbed. Take the pan off the heat and let it rest for 5 minutes. Remove the lid and fluff the rice. It's ready to serve.

For the Vegetable Pan Roast:

3   tablespoons unsalted butter

1   tablespoon balsamic vinegar

1   tablespoon soy sauce

16 medium-size shiitake mushrooms, cut in half

½   cup sweet corn kernels, fresh or frozen

1½ red bell peppers, stemmed, seeded, and cut into irregular ½-inch-square pieces

1   cup vine-ripe cherry tomatoes

4   medium-size handfuls baby spinach

Start cooking the Vegetable Pan Roast 4 minutes before the salmon fillets are finished cooking by melting the butter in a 12-inch sauté pan until it's hot but not burning. Mix together the balsamic vinegar and soy sauce and set aside. Add the mushrooms to the pan and sauté for 1 minute, tossing them once. Add the corn, red bell peppers, and cherry tomatoes and cook on high for 2 minutes, tossing once. To finish the pan roast, toss in the spinach and the balsamic soy drizzle. Cook on high heat for 1 minute, tossing once. Serve.

For the Salmon:

4   teaspoons Peppery Orange Aioli (see page 27)

To cook the salmon fillets, coat each fillet with a teaspoon of Peppery Orange Aioli. Begin grilling the fillets on a medium-hot charbroiler for about 3 minutes per side. Give each fillet a quarter turn on the first side to get nice grill marks. Don't overcook the salmon. It can be cooked through but still be moist. If you don't have a charbroiler, pan sear the fish in a lightly oiled large sauté pan. The cooking time is about the same.

To serve the dish, spread about ¾ cup of the hot Spanish Rice around each of four warm dinner plates. Place a salmon fillet just off center over the rice and spoon equal portions of the Vegetable Pan Roast around the fish. Garnish the dish with fresh herb sprigs. I think a little of the Horseradish Sour Cream Drizzle (see page 172) goes great with this salmon, so if you want to try it, drizzle a little over the dish and enjoy.

Fresh Alaskan Halibut, Mediterranean Style

This dish is an experience of a little coastal village along the sea. Maybe you've been there.

Makes 4 servings

Menu:

Mediterranean Salad

Saffron-Lemon Risotto

Warm Heirloom Tomato Orange Broth (see page 180)

4   6-ounce fresh Alaskan halibut fillets

For the Mediterranean Salad:

1   ripe avocado

2   Minneola tangerines or a large naval orange, peeled, cored, and cut into wedges

½   small red onion, sliced thin across the grain

16 pitted kalamata olives

2   small fennel bulbs, boiled until tender and then thinly sliced

1   red bell pepper, stemmed , seeded, and cut in thin strips lengthwise

2   tablespoons freshly snipped basil

2   tablespoons extra-virgin olive oil

1   tablespoon freshly squeezed lemon juice

Pinch kosher salt and fresh ground black pepper

Make the salad just before serving the fish. Cut the avocado into quarters, remove the pit, and set aside. Put the rest of the salad ingredients into a bowl and toss gently so they are coated with the olive oil and lemon.

For the Saffron-Lemon Risotto:

2   tablespoons olive oil

½   medium yellow onion, diced

1½ cups Arborio rice, uncooked

1   teaspoon finely grated lemon zest

½   cup dry white wine

4   cups boiling chicken stock

2   tablespoons unsalted butter

½   cup grated Parmesan cheese

To make the rice, heat up the olive oil in an oval saucepan and add the diced onion. Sauté for 2 minutes. Add the rice and lemon zest and stir them into the onion. Sauté for 1 minute. Add the white wine and stir the rice until most of the wine is absorbed. Add hot chicken broth a ladle at a time and stir the rice. Stirring is the key to bringing out the creaminess of the risotto. As the liquid is absorbed, add more stock and keep stirring. Continue this process until the rice has a nice creaminess but is still al dente. In other words the rice should have a little bite to it. Stir in the butter and the Parmesan. The rice is ready to serve. Try to time this process so the rice is done when the fish is finished cooking.

For the Warm Heirloom Tomato Orange Broth:

1 cup Heirloom Tomato Salad (see page 65)

1 tablespoon unsalted butter

   Juice from ½ Minneola tangerine or navel orange

To make the broth, simply put the ingredients in a small saucepan over medium-low heat and let them warm up right before you serve the dish. Let everything melt together at a slow simmer and then stop cooking. It's ready to use.

For the Halibut:

4 teaspoons Peppery Orange Aioli (see page 27)

1 tablespoon ground fennel seed and coriander seed mixed together

To finish the dish, first cook the halibut. Rub the fish with the Peppery Orange Aioli and sprinkle with the ground fennel and coriander seed mixture. You can either pan sear the halibut in a large sauté pan or charbroil the fish on your grill. It will

take about 5 minutes per side if the halibut is quite thick. You be the judge. While the fish is cooking, you can finish the salad.

When the halibut is finished cooking, serve the dish. I like to serve this in large, warm pasta bowls. In each of four warm bowls, spoon equal portions of the Warm Heirloom Tomato Orange Broth. Then put in a nice mound of risotto. Put a halibut fillet just off center into the risotto. Put an avocado wedge next to the halibut fillet and spoon the Mediterranean Salad over the avocado wedge. Sprinkle the dish with freshly snipped basil and it is ready to serve. Enjoy the food and enjoy life.

desserts

■■■■

I love to make desserts. A secret part of me would just like to have a little dessert shop around the corner on an intimate street. I would call it Mountain Decadence and I would make my ice creams and tarts and strudels and bread puddings and pour my sauces over them and it would smell like chocolate and caramelized sugar and be a little steamy and inviting on a cold day.

When Sheila and I traveled in France we noticed that everywhere we went, large city or small village, the dessert shops and bistros and little hole-in-the-wall food stands were full of similar versions of traditional desserts. Apple tarts were everywhere. Each shop in each region had its own unique style. Floating islands, fresh berry pastries, chocolate confections, light buttery flaky pastries with rich creamy fillings. They were amazingly beautiful, always fresh and inviting. It struck us that the people there must eat a lot of dessert and that it must be important in their lives to have these wonderful sweet treats in full view and available at all times. If culture is what we imagine and then produce, I like that culture we experienced in France. I'm sure that all people that travel and experience other visions of life bring some of it home with them. I know that we did.

The Delights of the Naked Stranger came to me all those years ago on that fateful trip to Aspen in 1968. I was leaving an old life behind and beginning the discovery of what I was to become. It came to me in the form of a poem I was writing on that trip, going through a much younger Las Vegas at four in the morning when I was very sleepy and writing in my notebook, which I tend to do a lot when I'm on road trips. The poem has long been lost and thank goodness. I'm sure it wasn't very good. But the line about "The Delights of the Naked Stranger" has stayed with me. One night in Crested Butte in 1976 at my restaurant, Soupcon, I decided to name a dessert The Delights of the Naked Stranger. The reaction I got was amazing. My customers loved the name. I've continued that tradition all these years. It means something a little different to each person. Maybe they are a little embarrassed but they always laugh or smile at the thought of it.

Mountain Decadence is the name I use for my ice creams: Mountain Decadence Ice Cream. It is also the term I use to describe my style and approach to food and mountain living. It implies the total enjoyment of the mountain life.

Here are Vintage desserts. They are my tradition. I hope you enjoy them. I'd like to start with our dessert sauces because you can have one on hand and use it with one of my desserts or just with ice cream or a piece of cake or fruit. Simple and easy, and it will add a nice touch.

■ ■ ■ ■

Caramel Sauce

The prince of sauces. The tang of burnt sugar and cream spells satisfaction.

Makes 2 cups

1   cup cream
½   cup unsalted butter
1   cup sugar
2   tablespoons water
2   teaspoons pure vanilla extract
2   tablespoons brandy or Calvados

To make caramel sauce, have the cup of cream measured and ready. Cut the butter in pieces. Put the sugar and water into a saucepan and turn up the heat to high. The water should dissolve the sugar fairly quickly. The mixture will begin to cook, and the idea is to burn the sugar slowly to a nice, rich, deep reddish-brown but not too dark or it will turn bitter. This may take a little practice but keep trying. The mixture is also very hot so be careful. Just before the sugar mixture gets to the desired color, take it off the heat and stir in the butter pieces. Slowly add the cream, being careful not to splatter.

Put the mixture back over a medium heat and continue simmering for a few minutes. The sugar may ball up a little but be patient as it will dissolve and the mixture will come together. When it does, bring it up to a simmer and add the vanilla extract and the brandy. Let it simmer 1 or 2 minutes more and remove it from the heat. The caramel sauce should be ready. It keeps great in the refrigerator for a week. Just reheat the amount you are going to use and pour it over ice cream, pool it under a piece of cake, or drizzle it over hot bread pudding. Apple cake and caramel sauce were made for each other.

CHOCOLATE SAUCE

This sauce is so mellow and rich it's hard not to eat it by the spoonful.

Makes 2½ cups

9 tablespoons unsalted butter

⅜ cup semisweet chocolate

¾ cup good quality cocoa powder

2¼ cups sugar

1 cup heavy cream

2 tablespoons liqueur like brandy, Grand Marnier, or Amaretto

½ teaspoon kosher salt

1 tablespoon pure vanilla extract

To make the sauce, melt the butter with the semi-sweet chocolate in a saucepan over moderate heat. Add the cocoa and sugar and blend. Stir in the cream. Increase the heat a little and bring the mixture up to a boil for 10 seconds. Add the brandy or other liqueur and simmer 1 minute. Remove from heat and stir in the salt and vanilla extract. It's ready to serve or you can cool it down and store in the refrigerator for a week. Just warm up the amount you need and serve. It's great on ice cream or as a pool under cake; it's doubly good combined with a spoonful of caramel sauce.

*I like pure Mexican vanilla with chocolate so try that if you can find some, or get some in Mexico if you make a trip down there.

HOT FUDGE SAUCE

This sauce is the blood brother of Chocolate Sauce. It's deeper, darker, lustier. It was made for ice cream and toasted nuts.

Makes about 2 cups

1 cup bittersweet chocolate, cut into small pieces

¼ cup orange blossom honey

½ cup light corn syrup

½ cup water

¾ cup good quality cocoa powder

2 teaspoons instant espresso coffee granules

3 tablespoons brandy or bourbon

To make this sauce, put the chocolate and the honey into a saucepan and melt together over low heat. Now add the remaining ingredients and blend thoroughly with a wire whip over moderate heat. Bring the mixture up to a nice simmer for a few minutes. Continue stirring the mixture throughout the process. It is finished when it's nice and smooth and fudgy.

PECAN BRANDY SAUCE

This dessert sauce brings a Southern punch to a dish of ice cream or a fresh peach shortcake. Try it over our bread pudding instead of whiskey sauce. You'll be hard-pressed to decide which one you like better. If you use brandy, it will be smoother. If you use bourbon it will rock!

Makes about 3 cups

2	cups dark brown sugar
½	cup butter
½	cup cream
¼	cup light corn syrup
½	cup brandy or bourbon
1	cup chopped toasted pecans

To make, put the first four ingredients into a saucepan and bring to a moderate boil for 5 minutes. Stir a few times. Turn off the heat and add the brandy or bourbon and the chopped toasted pecans. Return to heat and boil for 1 minute. It's ready to serve warm or at room temperature. Stores great in the refrigerator for a week, tightly covered.

WHISKEY SABAYON

The crème de la crème of dessert sauces. This sauce is the essence of New Orleans and was invented to pour over bread pudding. But I love it over warm gingerbread or a rich butter cake. You can substitute fresh lemon juice for the whiskey and have a great lemon sabayon to pour over your favorite slice of cake. With fresh berries, the cake, the lemon sabayon, some whipped cream, and powdered sugar, you are now experiencing Mountain Decadence at its best.

Makes about 2 cups

1	cup sugar
2	tablespoons water
1	egg
½	cup unsalted butter, melted
½	cup good Kentucky bourbon

Make the sauce by adding the sugar and water to a small stainless steel bowl and placing it over a pot of simmering water. With a wire whisk, stir in the egg and continue to stir for 3 or 4 minutes until the mixture is smooth and creamy. The sabayon will be thickened and a pale yellow color. Stir in the melted butter. When it is thoroughly incorporated, remove the mixture from the heat and stir in the bourbon. Continue whisking until the mixture is fully blended. This sauce will have a nice kick to it. On a special note: Not only can you substitute lemon juice for the bourbon, you can also substitute another liqueur. Try Amaretto or Grand Marnier. They work great. Sauce stores for a week in the refrigerator.

Bachelors' Berries and Brandy Berry Sauce

This is one of the simplest and best dessert condiments you can have on hand. It goes great over ice cream, as a complement to crème brûlée, or as an accompaniment to cake. You can make it with either fresh or frozen berries and store it in your refrigerator year-round. And the juice becomes my Brandy Berry Sauce. It's always great to have something that is easy and delicious. This is one of those things.

Makes 5 cups

4   pints berries, such as raspberries, black-berries, blueberries, strawberries, or a combination

1½   cups sugar

1½   cups brandy

To make, simply put the berries in a bowl. Pour over the sugar and the brandy. Stir it all up gently and store it in a big glass jar or bowl. The juices of the berries will blend with the sugar and brandy to form a very delicious and versatile dessert condiment. Cover tightly and store in the refrigerator.

Homemade ice cream is one of the special treats of life. Here are four of my ice creams that you can easily make at home. I use ice cream as an element of many of my desserts. What better combination than a piece of warm strawberry strudel and a dollop of ice cream with a drizzle of caramel sauce?

■■■■

MOUNTAIN DECADENCE WHITE CHOCOLATE ICE CREAM

When you make this ice cream, use a French or Swiss white chocolate. I use Callebaut or Cocoa Barry. These chocolates have more cocoa butter than American versions and are richer, smoother, and tastier.

Makes 2½ quarts

1   quart whole milk

1   quart heavy cream

2   cups sugar

18 ounces white chocolate, cut in pieces

3   tablespoons pure vanilla extract

12 egg yolks, blended together with a wire whisk

To make this ice cream, place the milk and cream in a stainless steel bowl over a pot of boiling water. Heat the mixture until it scalds, which is when a film begins to form over the mixture. Now add the sugar, white chocolate, and vanilla extract. Stir the mixture from time to time as the chocolate melts. When the chocolate has totally melted and the mixture is nice and hot, slowly pour in the egg yolks, whisking constantly. Continue cooking the ice cream mixture for about 15 minutes, stirring often with the whisk.

The mixture will thicken up a bit and be nice and creamy.

Remove the bowl from over the steaming pot and let it begin to cool on a counter. Transfer to the refrigerator to get it really cold. When it is cold, you can make the ice cream in your ice cream freezer according to the manufacturer's instructions. When it is finished, put the ice cream in a container and then into your freezer. It will take a few hours to finish hardening so it is scoopable. It will last a long time in your freezer, but you will eat it before very long!

MOUNTAIN DECADENCE CRÈME BRÛLÉE ICE CREAM

This is my ice cream version of a crème brûlée. It's the essence of lusty eating and goes great with any flaky pastry fruit tart or strudel.

Makes 2½ quarts

1   quart whole milk

1   quart heavy cream

1   cup sugar

12   egg yolks

3   tablespoons pure vanilla extract

1½   cups sugar

To make this ice cream, place the milk and cream in a stainless steel bowl over a pot of boiling water. Let the mixture heat up until a film forms over the cream. Now add the cup of sugar, egg yolks, and vanilla extract. Stir the mixture with a wire whisk.

While the mixture is cooking, caramelize the 1½ cups of sugar. Place the sugar in a saucepan with 2 tablespoons of water and turn up the heat to moderately high. The sugar will dissolve in the water and then begin to burn. It is a controlled burn, so if it is darkening too fast turn down the heat a little. You want the sugar to caramelize to a nice, rich brown color. Don't let it turn black. It is now very hot so be careful. With a towel to protect your hand, pour the caramelized sugar into the ice cream mixture. It will splatter so stand back a little. Stir the caramelized sugar into the mixture until it is thoroughly blended in. Stir the mixture over the water bath for a few more minutes and it should be done.

Remove the bowl from the steaming pot and let it cool down. Place it in the refrigerator and let it get cold. Follow the freezing instructions for the white chocolate ice cream to finish it off (see page 189).

On a special note: I have two variations of this ice cream I just love. The first is to add the fine grated zest of one large orange to the ice cream mixture during the cooking process. This will impart an orange flavor to the brûlée ice cream to make Burnt Orange Ice Cream. I got the idea for this ice cream after John Prine came out with his Burnt Orange Album, which I loved, and knew I just had to make Burnt Orange Ice Cream. The other variation is to stir into the finished Crème Brûlée recipe about 1½ cups toasted chopped pecans before you put the ice cream into your refrigerator. You will then have Mountain Decadence Toasted Pecan Brûlée Ice Cream and it is wonderful.

MOUNTAIN DECADENCE ORGANIC BANANA ICE CREAM

I use organic bananas because they are richer and creamier tasting than normal bananas. Let these bananas sit out at room temperature for a few days and become overripe. That brings out the sugars and intensifies the flavor of the bananas. This ice cream will blow your mind!

Makes 2½ quarts

1½	cups whole milk
1½	cups heavy cream
1	cup sugar
½	cup orange blossom honey
1	tablespoon pure vanilla extract
10	egg yolks
8	overripe bananas
½	cup sour cream

To make the ice cream, place the milk and cream in a stainless steel bowl and put the bowl over a pot of boiling water. Heat the mixture until it scalds, which is when a film begins to form over the mixture, and then add the sugar, honey, vanilla extract and then the egg yolks, stirring with a wire whisk as you add the yolks. Cook this mixture for about 5 minutes over the pot of steaming water, then remove the bowl to a counter and let cool.

Now you can finish the ice cream. Get out your food processor and in batches process the cream mixture with the bananas and the sour cream. Process each batch until it is smooth and creamy. When you are finished you can freeze the ice cream in your ice cream maker according to the manufacturer's instructions.

MOUNTAIN DECADENCE CRÈME FRAICHE ICE CREAM

Crème fraiche is the cultured heavy cream of France. It is rich, slightly cheesy, and has a delicious tartness to it that explodes in your mouth. It is very easy to make the crème fraiche. It makes unreal ice cream, but you can also use it to spoon over berries or peaches and sprinkle with a little sugar, or use it to enliven a sauce. I've had crème fraiche in France served with fromage blanc, which is a molded white goat cheese. You pour the crème fraiche over the fromage blanc and sprinkle it with sugar. Talk about a double rich whammy. And the people are slim and trim. I love a culture that can do that.

Makes 1¾ quarts

For the Crème Fraiche:

1   cup cultured buttermilk

4   cups heavy cream

For the Ice Cream:

4   egg yolks

¾   cup sugar

1   recipe Crème Fraiche

½   teaspoon pure vanilla extract

¾   cup light corn syrup

You have to make this recipe a couple of days ahead of when you want to serve it. To make the crème fraiche, mix the buttermilk with the cream. I like to put the mixture into a clean wine carafe, cover it with clear plastic wrap, and let it sit out at room temperature overnight. The cream will thicken up a lot like yogurt. The next day put the carafe in your refrigerator for two days to let the flavors develop and become thick and tart.

To make the ice cream, in a large bowl beat the egg yolks and the sugar with a wire whisk for a few minutes until they turn a nice creamy yellow color. Add the remaining ingredients and blend thoroughly. Now you can make the ice cream in your ice cream maker according to the manufacturer's instructions. Store in your freezer and get ready for the best ice cream you've ever had.

Note: This is an uncooked ice cream mixture so we use ultrapasteurized egg yolks. Ask your grocer to order you some.

Here is a special ice cream tip. If you don't have the time or the inclination to make your own ice cream, you can make up your own flavors from store-bought ice cream. Here are some examples, and they are delicious. Use your own imagination to come up with your own new flavors. The possibilities are endless.

■■■■

NEW ORLEANS COFFEE—TOASTED PECAN ICE CREAM

Makes 1 quart

1   quart good quality coffee ice cream
1   tablespoon pure vanilla extract
1   tablespoon bourbon
1   tablespoon brown sugar
¾   cup chopped toasted pecans

Soften ice cream just enough to blend in other ingredients. Fold in vanilla, bourbon, brown sugar, and pecans. Refreeze the mixture and you'll have an amazing treat. By the way, my favorite coffee ice cream is Starbucks Classic Coffee. Try it!

MEXICAN VANILLA ICE CREAM

Makes 1 quart

1   quart good quality vanilla ice cream
1   tablespoon pure Mexican vanilla extract

Soften ice cream just enough to blend in vanilla. Fold in Mexican vanilla and thoroughly blend. Pure Mexican vanilla extract has a rich big flavor. Do not use an imitation. Refreeze the mixture.

SICILIAN VANILLA ICE CREAM

Makes 1 quart

1   quart good quality vanilla ice cream
¼   teaspoon ground cinnamon
2   tablespoons Sicilian Crème de Marsala
¾   cup chopped toasted walnuts

I also call this ice cream Silly Vanilla. Soften ice cream just enough to blend in other ingredients. Add cinnamon, Sicilian Crème de Marsala, and walnuts. Blend thoroughly and refreeze.

CHOCOLATE CHUNK BREAD PUDDING WITH STEAMY WHISKEY SABAYON SAUCE

This dish is comfort food at its best. It is beyond trendy—it will never go out of style and will come through for you whenever you need a great dessert. Enjoy the aroma of steaming whiskey and cinnamon that will fill the room.

Makes 8 servings

10 ounces French baguette, cut in 1-inch square pieces

3½ cups whole milk

4   whole eggs plus 1 egg yolk

1½ cups sugar

1   tablespoon ground cinnamon

2   tablespoons pure vanilla extract

1½ cups large semisweet chocolate chunks

4   tablespoons unsalted butter, melted

Whiskey Sabayon Sauce (see page 187)

Preheat oven to 375 degrees F. Put the bread squares into a stainless steel bowl and add the milk. Let the bread soak up all the milk. When the bread becomes soft, crumble it up into a nice even texture. In another bowl combine the eggs, egg yolk, sugar, cinnamon, and vanilla. Using a wire whisk, blend the ingredients until they are smooth. Now stir in the chocolate chunks.

Add the bread mixture to the egg mixture and stir until well blended. Brush eight 6-ounce ramekins with melted butter. Fill each ramekin three-fourths full with the bread pudding mixture, and then pour 1 teaspoon of melted butter over each bread pudding. Place the ramekins into a shallow baking pan that is filled with 1 inch of water. Bake in the preheated oven for about 45 minutes or until the puddings are puffed up and firm to the touch.

While the puddings are baking, make the Whiskey Sabayon Sauce.

Chocolate Chunk Bread Pudding is great served immediately unmolded on individual serving plates with 2 to 3 tablespoons of Whiskey Sabayon poured over the top. Or, you can let the puddings cool down to serve later. If serving later, simply unmold each pudding onto an individual ovenproof serving plate. When ready to serve, heat for 5 minutes in an oven at 425 degrees F. When you remove the pudding from the oven, it (along with the plate) will be very hot. To serve, place the hot bread pudding plate onto a larger cool plate so nobody gets burned. Ladle the Whiskey Sabayon over each pudding and serve. The whiskey will steam up and make everyone a bit light-headed, which is the objective anyway, after all!

Vintage –

1 9 5

The Delights of the Naked Stranger

Just what are the delights, and who is the naked stranger? We all have to figure that one out for ourselves, but it is fun to think about. In dessert parlance, it is decadent elements put together to form a special dish. And you've got all the elements right in the palm of your hand. Chocolate Sauce, Caramel Sauce, Bachelors' Berries, Mountain Decadence Ice Cream, and last but not least, Chocolate Truffle Torte. My first assistant cook in Sun Valley twenty years ago taught me how to make this torte. Her name is Buncy Jeffrey and she came out of the blue right when I needed somebody good. She was there in the nick of time when my restaurant was under big pressure. Later she saved me again when I had a bad horse accident and was out for an entire summer. Buncy took over the kitchen and with able assistance from Lynn Welker, saved the day—or should I say the summer. To these women, I say thank you! I've had many versions of The Delights over the years, but this one is the best.

Makes 16 servings

For the Torte Crust:

- 1 cup lightly toasted pecans
- ½ cup sugar
- 4½ tablespoons unsalted butter, melted

For the Chocolate Truffle Filling:

- 2½ cups semisweet good quality chocolate, cut in pieces
- ½ cup unsalted butter, cut in 6 pieces
- 2 cups heavy cream
- 6 tablespoons sugar
- Pinch salt
- 6 tablespoons brandy

To make the crust, put the pecans and sugar in a food processor and process for a few seconds. Add the butter and process again for a few seconds. Everything should be evenly blended. Now press this mixture into the bottom of a 10-inch springform cake pan allowing for a ¼-inch rim around the inside of the springform. Bake the crust for about 12 minutes at 350 degrees F. The baking pecans and butter will smell delicious. Remove the crust from the oven and let cool.

To make the filling, place the chocolate and the butter in a stainless steel bowl over a simmering pot of water. Let the chocolate melt slowly with the butter, stirring until well blended. Remove the bowl from the heat. Meanwhile, put the cream, sugar, and pinch of salt into a saucepan and bring up to almost a boil. Stir a few times to make sure the sugar dissolves. Turn off the heat for a few seconds and add the brandy. Turn on the heat and bring the mixture up to a boil for a few seconds. Don't let it boil over. Remove from heat immediately. Pour the cream mixture into the chocolate mixture and blend thoroughly until it is perfectly smooth. Be sure to taste it, just don't drink it all! Pour the truffle mixture into the pecan crust. Put the torte in the refrigerator for at least 4 hours to firm it up. It now becomes the most delicious chocolate candy that you can cut slices of. Unmold the torte before serving; take it out of the cooler about an hour before you are going to slice it.

To assemble The Delights of the Naked Stranger, on individual serving plates, place a small pool of warmed Chocolate Sauce (see page 186) beside a small pool of warmed Caramel Sauce (see page 185). Cut a slice of the torte about 1 inch wide at the outer edge of the slice and place it on the pool of Caramel Sauce. Put a scoop of Mountain Decadence Ice Cream (see pages 189–192) on the pool of Chocolate Sauce. Now garnish the dish with a tablespoon of Bachelors' Berries (see page 188) with the berry juice. Serve the dish and maybe this will be your lucky night.

BLOOD ORANGE DEMITASSE CRÈME BRÛLÉE

Blood Orange is one of the many citrus crèmes brûlées that I make. The key to making a citrus brûlée is in using the finely grated zest of the skin instead of using the juice. So follow the recipe for the Blood Orange Crème Brûlée, but realize you can also substitute the zest of a navel orange, lemon, lime, key lime, or tangerine for the blood orange zest. These brûlées are refreshing and silky smooth, and you will be pleased with the variety of flavors you will have at your fingertips. I make my Crème Brûlée in demitasse espresso cups because they make a very nice small dessert. I accompany the brûlée with a side of our Bachelors' Berries for a fabulous taste and texture contrast.

Makes 6 to 7 servings

3	large fresh egg yolks
I	demitasse cup sugar
I	tablespoon finely grated blood orange zest
	A few drops pure vanilla extract
I½	cups heavy cream
3 to 3½	teaspoons sugar

To make the brûlée, preheat oven to 300 degrees F. In a bowl, beat the egg yolks and the sugar with a wire whisk until they are a creamy pale yellow. This will take 2 or 3 minutes. Add blood orange zest, vanilla extract, and cream and thoroughly blend with the whisk.

Place 6 or 7 demitasse espresso cups into a shallow baking pan and fill the cups with the brûlée mixture. Fill the pan with warm water about two-thirds up the sides of the brûlée cups and place the baking pan in the oven. Cook the brûlées for about 35 to 40 minutes in the oven. Check them a few times during the cooking process because on some days they get done faster than on others. They are done when the brûlée mixture is firm and a little puffed. Take the pan out of the oven and let the brûlées rest a while and cool down enough so you can remove them from the pan. Place them on a plate and put them in the refrigerator for a few hours so they set up nicely and become cold.

Now for the fun part. When you want to serve the brûlées, remove them from the fridge and sprinkle each with ½ teaspoon granulated sugar. Now you need a small propane torch that you can buy at your hardware store. Light it up and burn the sugar on top of each brûlée. Don't be afraid! It's a small, luscious, silky dessert, so have fun with it.

Mexican Vanilla Demitasse Crème Brûlée

Here is another way to use Mexican vanilla and it is simplicity to the max.

Makes 6 to 7 servings

3   large fresh egg yolks

1   demitasse cup sugar

1   tablespoon real Mexican vanilla extract

1½ cups heavy cream

3 to 3½ teaspoons sugar

To make this brûlée, simply beat the egg yolks with the sugar and the vanilla extract in a bowl until they are smooth, creamy, and somewhat thickened. Add the heavy cream and mix thoroughly. Now follow the cooking and serving instructions for the Blood Orange Demitasse Crème Brûlée (see page 199). Enjoy a taste of Mexico.

Catalan Demitasse Crème Brûlée

Here are the flavors of a tiny hidden region on the Mediterranean between Spain and France, captured in a little demitasse espresso cup about the size of Catalonia itself. The taste of a culture captured in a cup—cool idea.

Makes 6 or 7 servings

3   large fresh egg yolks

1   demitasse cup sugar

½   teaspoon pure vanilla extract, Mexican preferred

¼   teaspoon whole fennel seed

1   teaspoon finely grated orange zest

½   teaspoon finely grated lemon zest

1½ cups heavy cream

3 to 3½ teaspoons sugar

To make Catalan Brûlée, beat the egg yolks and the sugar together in a bowl until they are smooth and creamy and somewhat thickened. Add the vanilla extract, fennel seed, orange zest, and lemon zest; beat for a few more seconds. This brings all the flavors out. Add the cream and blend thoroughly. Follow the cooking and serving instructions for the Blood Orange Demitasse Crème Brûlée (see page 199).

White Chocolate Toasted Pecan Ice Cream Balls with Hot Fudge Sauce

A great simple dessert. I love to coat scoops of ice cream with toasted nuts and serve them in a pool of Chocolate, Caramel, or Hot Fudge Sauce. Here is one of my favorite versions.

Makes 2 to 3 servings

1   cup chopped toasted pecans

Hot Fudge Sauce (see page 186)

Mountain Decadence White Chocolate
Ice Cream, 2 scoops per serving
(see page 189)

To make the dish, chop the pecans and toast them in an oven set to 350 degrees F for about 6 or 7 minutes. Cool them to room temperature before proceeding. Warm up some Hot Fudge Sauce and have it ready. To serve, put the pecans in a large enough bowl to add a scoop of ice cream. Add ice cream scoop and roll it around in the nuts, pressing it lightly into the nuts so they stick to the ice cream. Make a pool of 2 to 3 tablespoons of warmed Hot Fudge Sauce on each serving plate and place two pecan-coated ice cream balls in the pool. You don't need to make the ice cream scoops too large as they get quite hefty when you coat them with the pecans. Use your own judgment as to size.

Jamaican Chimney Sweeps Gelato

In Italy there is a traditional ice cream dessert called the Chimney Sweeps Gelato. It is made with the very traditional egg custard gelato, bourbon, and fresh ground espresso. You pour a bottle cap or two of bourbon over the gelato and then sprinkle the dish with ground espresso. What a great little dessert, and it's oh-so-potent. I, of course, came up with my own unique versions of this dish. Here is one of my favorites.

Makes 4 servings

8   scoops Mountain Decadence Organic
       Banana Ice Cream (see page 191) or use
       store-bought ice cream

4 to 8 bottle caps of Dark Jamaican rum

       Several pinches of fresh ground espresso

To assemble the dish, simply place 2 scoops of the ice cream into each of four ice cream dishes. Pour over 1 or 2 bottle caps of rum and sprinkle with some fresh ground espresso. Get ready for a jolt of Jamaica. A variation on this is to use 1 scoop of banana ice cream and 1 scoop of coconut ice cream. I call that dish the Piña Colada Chimney.

Italian Coffee Chimney Sweeps Gelato

For those of you who just can't get enough coffee, this version of the Chimney Sweeps will do you justice. It is close to the traditional Italian Chimney but with a double dose of coffee.

Makes 4 servings

8   scoops of your favorite coffee ice cream
4 to 8 bottle caps of Kentucky bourbon
   Several pinches of fresh ground espresso

To assemble the dish, place 2 scoops of coffee ice cream into each of four ice cream dishes. Pour 1 or 2 bottle caps of bourbon over the ice cream and sprinkle with some fresh ground espresso. This dessert will wake you up!

Fresh Pear Strudel

Fruit strudels have become a forgotten dessert in the United States. I don't see them around much anymore. But I love a good strudel. It is buttery and flaky phyllo pastry with soft creamy fruit on the inside. Served warm with a scoop of ice cream, it is a wonderful way to end a meal.

Makes 10 servings

For the Filling:

1   pound fresh pears, peeled and sliced

¼   cup dried Zante black currants

¼   cup lightly toasted chopped pecans

¼   teaspoon ground cinnamon

1   cup sugar

1   teaspoon finely grated lemon zest

    Juice of ½ lemon

For the Phyllo Pastry:

1   cup finely ground saltine cracker crumbs

½   cup ground toasted pecans

½   cup brown sugar

½   cup unsalted butter, melted

10 (12- x 17-inch) phyllo sheets

Preheat oven to 375 degrees F.

To assemble the strudel, peel and slice the pears, discarding the cores. Put the sliced pears and the rest of the filling ingredients in a mixing bowl and fold together gently. Set aside.

Mix the ground saltine crumbs, pecans, and brown sugar together in a small bowl and set aside. Melt the butter and have it ready. Brush a baking sheet with a light coating of melted butter.

On a clean, dry counter with lots of room, place the 10 sheets of phyllo dough. Place a lightly damp cloth over the phyllo so it doesn't dry out. Place 2 of the phyllo sheets, one on top of the other, to the side of the stack of phyllo sheets. Brush the top one with melted butter and sprinkle lightly with the cracker and pecan crumb mixture. Repeat by stacking 2 sheets of phyllo at a time and brushing with butter and then sprinkling with the crumbs until you've used all 10 phyllo sheets. You now have a nice stack of phyllo sheets with the crumbs in between.

With a large spoon, spoon the filling evenly inside the long edge of the phyllo stack. Use all of the filling. Gently but firmly roll up the phyllo stack like a big cigar. With two spatulas placed under each end of the strudel, lift the strudel and place it diagonally onto the baking sheet. Using a serrated bread knife, score the strudel with diagonal slices about 1¼ inches apart. This will be where you slice each serving. Brush the entire strudel with the melted butter. Place the strudel on a mid-level rack in the oven and bake for about 30 minutes. As the strudel bakes, juices will run out onto the baking sheet. I like to spoon these juices over the strudel as it cooks. The strudel will be a beautiful golden brown and crispy on the outside when it is finished. Remove from the oven and let it rest for about 15 minutes. Serve it warm. Slice it along the scoring marks. It's great with whipped cream and a snowstorm of powdered sugar. It's also delicious served with a drizzle of Caramel Sauce (see page 185) and a scoop of Mountain Decadence White Chocolate or Crème Brûlée Ice Cream (see pages 189 and 190).

You can make the strudel ahead of time to serve later. Just remember to remove it from the baking sheet when it comes out of the oven before it cools off or it will stick very badly to the baking sheet. Warm up whatever portion you want to serve for about 5 minutes in the oven at 350 degrees F before serving.

One last note: the leftover strudel is great in the morning for breakfast with a hot cup of coffee or tea.

FRESH STRAWBERRY STRUDEL

I love strawberry strudel. But I love it without currents or pecans in the mixture. Just the pure essence of strawberries is what I want. It is like an exotic perfume and goes straight to the pleasure centers of your brain.

Makes 10 servings

For the Filling:

1¼ pounds ripe strawberries

½ teaspoon ground cinnamon

1 cup sugar

1 teaspoon finely grated lemon zest

1 tablespoon freshly squeezed lemon juice

For the Phyllo Pastry:

1 cup finely ground saltine cracker crumbs

½ cup ground toasted pecans

½ cup brown sugar

½ cup unsalted butter, melted

10 (12- x 17-inch) phyllo sheets

Preheat oven to 375 degrees F.

　　To assemble, bake, and serve, follow the instructions for the Fresh Pear Strudel (see page 206). The process is exactly the same. Also it works great to substitute other fruits for the fruit in either of these strudels. Peaches, apples, and nectarines all work well.

MACADAMIA NUT TOFFEE TART

This dessert has been popular in my restaurants for twenty years. In that way it has become a tradition much like apple tart in France. That's a great feeling. The tart is like a warm nutty candy bar. It is great served fresh and warm with a dollop of ice cream to melt over it. It is also delicious the next day cut in slivers and dunked in hot coffee for breakfast. It's definitely a stylish power bar and a great energy boost any time of day. Here's how I make it.

Makes 8 to 10 servings

For the Pastry Crust:

2   cups good quality organic unbleached white flour

4   tablespoons sugar

¾   cup unsalted butter, cut in chunks

2   fresh egg yolks

1   tablespoon finely grated lemon zest

1   teaspoon fresh lemon juice

For the Filling:

1¼   cups heavy cream

1¼   cups sugar

1   teaspoon finely grated lemon zest

¼   teaspoon salt

¼   teaspoon pure vanilla extract

2   cups whole macadamia nuts, toasted to a light golden brown

Preheat oven to 375 degrees F. To make the crust, put the flour, sugar, and butter into a food processor and pulse until evenly mixed. Add the egg yolks, lemon zest, and lemon juice and pulse the processor just until the mixture becomes crumbly and starts to come together. Pour the mixture into an 11-inch fluted tart pan with a removable bottom and press the dough evenly over the bottom and sides of the pan. Bake the shell for about 10 minutes in the oven. Remove from the oven and, with a fork, evenly press down the pastry in the bottom of the tart pan. Let it cool.

In a saucepan, combine the heavy cream, sugar, lemon zest, salt, and vanilla extract. Bring the mixture to a boil while stirring. Reduce the heat and simmer for 5 minutes, stirring often. Add the macadamia nuts and cook 2 more minutes. Pour the mixture into the tart crust and place in the oven. Bake for about 40 minutes or until the tart has turned a luscious golden color, the toffee mixture is set, and the surface is nice and shiny. Remove from the oven to cool on the counter. As soon as the tart has cooled enough for you to handle, separate the tart and removable bottom from the tart pan. If you don't, the tart will stick to the sides and be very hard to separate. Let the tart cool for about an hour and then you will be able to cut it into nice slices for serving. We warm each slice for a minute before serving and I like to serve it with a dollop of Mountain Decadence Ice Cream (see pages 189 to 192).

Frozen Key Lime Soufflé

When it's hot outside this is a perfect dessert. The taste is bright and refreshing and the soufflé looks great. It's also fun to substitute other citrus ingredients for the lime juice and zest so you have a wide range of possible flavors. Try Mineola tangerine, lemon, and blood orange, or make a triple citrus soufflé using three different citrus ingredients together.

Makes 8 servings

- 8 homemade parchment paper sleeves
- 16 2-inch pieces of masking tape
- 8 6-ounce soufflé cups
- 1 cup sugar
- ¼ cup water
- 8 medium-size fresh egg yolks
- ½ cup fresh key lime juice
- 2 teaspoons finely grated key lime zest
- 2 cups heavy cream, whipped to soft peaks
- 2 tablespoons finely grated lime zest for garnish
- Whipped cream for garnish
- Fresh berries for garnish

The first thing to do is to make the parchment paper sleeves. Make these sleeves 4 inches high by 12 inches wide. Wrap a sleeve around each soufflé cup and secure it with two pieces of masking tape. Set them aside

To make the soufflé mixture, combine the sugar and water in a medium saucepan and cook over medium-high heat until the mixture reaches the soft ball stage, which registers 240 degrees on a candy thermometer. Mix the egg yolks in a blender. With the blender on high, add the sugar mixture slowly and mix well. Transfer the mixture to the bowl of an electric mixer and beat at medium speed until the mixture is cool. Add the lime juice and lime zest and blend well. Gently fold in the whipped cream with a rubber spatula. Spoon the mixture into each of the sleeved soufflé cups. Put the soufflés into the freezer at least 4 hours before serving.

To serve the soufflés, remove the parchment sleeve and press a little of the lime zest around the sides of the soufflé, top with a dollop of whipped cream, and sprinkle with a few fresh berries. Serve on a dessert plate with a doily. And remember to try other citrus fruits with this recipe. Enjoy!

White Chocolate Mousse with Toasted Hazelnuts

When I make this dessert I'm transported to the Swiss Alps. It's so much fun traveling around the world in your own kitchen. The cost of the food pays for your ticket, and your imagination puts the feeling in your bones. And the great thing is that you can go anywhere your desire takes you. Bon voyage!

Makes 6 or 7 servings

¾ cup fine Swiss or French white chocolate

⅓ cup warm milk

2 egg whites

1 cup heavy cream

3 to 4 tablespoons lightly toasted and chopped skinless hazelnuts

Fresh raspberries for garnish

Semisweet or dark chocolate shavings for garnish

To make this dessert, melt the white chocolate in a stainless steel bowl over a pan of gently simmering water. Add the warm milk, stirring until blended and smooth. Remove from heat and cool to room temperature. Beat egg whites until stiff peaks form. Fold egg whites gently into chocolate mixture with a rubber spatula. Whip the cream in a cold mixing bowl until beautiful whipped-cream clouds form; then fold them gently into the chocolate mixture until fully blended. Fold in the 3 to 4 tablespoons chopped hazelnuts.

Spoon the mousse into champagne glasses about two-thirds to three-fourths full. Cover each glass with a piece of clear plastic wrap and chill in the refrigerator for at least 3 hours or overnight. To serve the mousse, garnish it with a few fresh raspberries and a little shaved semisweet or dark chocolate.

The World's Best Root Beer Float

For this dessert we're staying right here in the good old USA. I'm being transported back to my high school days at Anaheim High in Southern California, where in the fall after football practice on blistering hot days we'd drag ourselves across the street from the high school to the local A&W Root Beer Drive In. It was an old classic high school hangout. We would be bruised, tired, and thirsty, and nothing quenched my thirst more than an A&W Root Beer float. It's one of my fondest high school memories.

Makes 1 serving

- 1   frozen and frosted soda glass
- 1   12-ounce can root beer (find an A&W for the authentic experience)
- 2   scoops of Mountain Decadence White Chocolate Ice Cream (see page 189)

Put the root beer into the frosted glass first. Add the ice cream. Let it rest a few seconds. Now dig in.

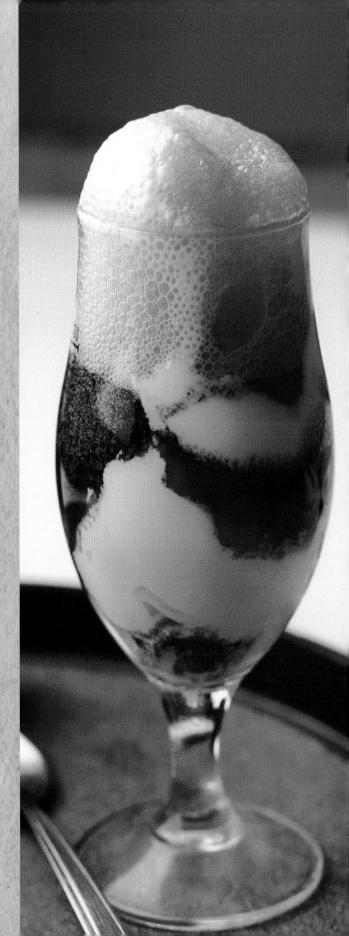

HONEY-GRILLED PEACHES WITH CRÈME FRAICHE ICE CREAM AND BRANDY BERRY SAUCE

Fresh ripe peaches grilled with a heavenly coating of caramelized sugar and honey must be the essence of summer. Don't try this dish with out-of-season fruit. It just won't work. Follow the fruit when it comes in season and is sweet and ripe. Peaches, nectarines, white peaches, and white nectarines. Just follow them through the summer. When summer is over remember how good they were and look forward to next year.

Makes 4 servings

- 4   ripe peaches
- 2   tablespoons sugar
-     Oil
- 8   teaspoons orange blossom honey (or your favorite honey)
- 4   teaspoons brandy or bourbon
- 8   tablespoons Brandy Berry Sauce from Bachelors' Berries (see page 188)
- 4   scoops Mountain Decadence Crème Fraiche Ice Cream (see page 192)

An hour before you will serve the dessert, cut the peaches in half, take out the pit, put them in a bowl face up, and sprinkle them with the sugar. To serve, very lightly oil the faces of the halved peaches and put them face-down on a medium-hot grill or BBQ. After 1 minute turn each peach ¼ turn and cook 1 more minute. Now turn the peaches over so the skin side is on the grill. Drizzle each peach face with the honey and the brandy or bourbon. Leave the peaches on the grill 1 or 2 more minutes. While the peaches are finishing, set up four dessert plates with 2 tablespoons each of the Brandy Berry Sauce and 1 scoop of Crème Fraiche Ice Cream. When the peaches are finished cooking place 2 halves on each plate by the ice cream and serve.

index

◼◼◼◼